Spring Forest
Level Two Manual

The course manual is for your personal use only.

Copyright 2002 Chunyi Lin. All worldwide rights are reserved and exclusively owned.

The "Yin-Yang Circle" with the "I Ching" marking is a trademark of Chunyi Lin and Spring Forest Qigong

Printed in the United States of America

Second Edition – November 2006

Notice: This manual and all Spring Forest Qigong teaching and learning materials are intended for your education of healthful practices. This manual and the other learning materials are not intended as a replacement for any medical treatment or therapy by a physician or other licensed health care provider. Rather, this manual and the other learning materials are intended to help you broaden your understanding of health and wellness and help you make informed choices of health options. Any application of the information in this manual and the other learning materials is at the student's discretion and sole responsibility.

Cover painting by Phyllis Jazdzewski © Chunyi Lin
Graphic design and layout by Jackie Anton
Cover design by Jim Hinman

www.springforestqigong.com

Table of Contents

Biography 4

Introduction 5

Learning Level Two 6

Being a Healer 7

Five Keys for Successful
Qigong Healing 10

Energy Systems of the Body
and Color Healing 20

General Healing Technique 23

The Healing Process
Step-by-Step 26

Healing 29

Small Universe 31

Detecting Blockages 33

Clear the Spine First 35

Special Healing Techniques 36

Addressing Specific Problems 57
   Head 57
   Shoulders and Neck 61
   Lungs 62
   Heart 63
   Liver 64
   Kidneys 64
   Female Breasts 65
   Areas related to the Kidneys ... 66
   Diabetes 66
   High & Low Blood Pressure ... 67
   High Cholesterol 68
   Heart Attack 68
   Constipation 68
   Diarrhea 68
   Digestion 69
   Cold, Flu, Fever, Sinus Problems,
   Asthma, and Emphysema 69
   Pregnancy &
   Menstrual Period 70
   Warts 70
   Arthritis 70
   Addictions 71

The Active Exercises 72

Practicing the Active
Exercises of Level Two 73
   Sword Fingers Practice 74
   Thunder Palms Practice 76
   10,000 Hands Practice 78
   Cloud Hands Practice 81
   Ending: Harvesting of Qi 82

Virtual Compass 83

Sitting Postures 85

Flexibility Exercises
for Sitting Postures 87

Hand Postures 89

Black Sesame Seeds 90

Closing Thoughts 91

Important Legal Warnings 93

On Discontinuing Medication 94

Biography

Chunyi Lin is a certified International Qigong Master and the creator and founder of Spring Forest Qigong. His fluency in numerous Chinese dialects provided him the rare opportunity to study with many of the most respected Qigong Masters in his native China. He has been teaching Qigong and using Qigong techniques to help others for more than twenty-five years. Master Lin is also a Tai Chi Master and highly skilled in Chinese herbal medicine and acupuncture.

Mr. Lin is the director of the Spring Forest Center for Health, Wellness & Empowerment in Minneapolis, MN. As many as 200 people, from across the United States and many foreign countries, come to his healing center for healing assistance and empowerment every week.

During 2004 he created an Educational Partnership with Normandale Community College of Bloomington, MN to provide fully accredited courses in Spring Forest Qigong health and healing techniques. All of the course curricula were created by Mr. Lin and he serves as the program director and lead instructor. Lin was formerly a college professor in Guangdon Province in China. In January of 2005, he was awarded a Masters Degree in Human Development-Holistic Health & Wellness from St. Mary's University in Minneapolis, MN. Lin served as Director of Qigong Programs at Anoka-Ramsey Community College in Anoka, Minnesota, from 1999 to 2004.

Master Lin teaches four levels of Spring Forest Qigong and has created a series of home learning materials for students, including videos, guided audio meditations and reference manuals. He is a frequent keynote speaker at national health conferences.

Since coming to the United States in 1995, he has helped thousands upon thousands of people to learn about the powerful, healing benefits of Spring Forest Qigong. He now devotes all of his time to the teaching of Spring Forest Qigong and helping others. He also sees people for private healing sessions. He lives in the Twin Cities.

His vision is "a healer in every family and a world without pain."

Introduction

Hello, my dear friend. Welcome to Spring Forest Qigong Level Two. As always, you will find my energy and the love energy of the universe with you.

Put yourself in a state of meditation and follow my words. Use your imagination and visualization and you will receive my energy better.

Today you are opening a door that will help you share the healing power of Spring Forest Qigong with your family and friends.

This manual will help you learn how to strengthen your own energy and how to do healing for a friend. You can help balance your friend's energy. I will show you how so many of my students are now able to detect energy blockages in other people, how they are able to remove these blockages, and give healing energy to help others. You can learn to do these things, too.

I hope you and your friends will find ample benefit from the practice of Spring Forest Qigong. Unfortunately, some people, even those I work with individually, do not experience the full benefit of Qigong. This is important to recognize if you or your friends are experiencing a current medical condition. I encourage you and your friends to try Qigong as a complementary practice to any current medical treatment. You or your friends should not make any decision to change current medical treatment without talking to a doctor or licensed health care provider.

Again, I very much hope that Spring Forest Qigong will provide many benefits to you and your friends, as it has for me and many, many other people.

Learning Level Two

I recommend you begin by flipping through this course manual and reading the headlines and subheads. This will familiarize you with the contents of Level Two.

Learning with a friend is also very helpful. That way you can practice what you are learning right away.

There is also a set of two videotapes that I highly recommend. I demonstrate my Level Two healing techniques on the video sessions along with the new Active Exercises for this level, the Virtual Compass so you can find the best direction for your practice, and tips for being able to sit in the Full Lotus position.

All of this information is also contained in this manual. The manual and video sessions are designed to complement each other.

Keep the course manual handy whenever you are practicing your healing. It is an excellent reference guide.

There is also a special Audio Session cassette that is available to assist you in practicing the Active Exercises of Level Two.

If you do not have these other learning tools, they are all available through our website at www.springforestqigong.com.

Being a Healer

To be a powerful and successful healer, you must know how to find out the cause of the sickness---the energy blockages, and then how to open up these blockages and how to give your friend healing energy. Remember, the body is healthy when the energy is balanced. Blockages cause imbalance, which can lead to sickness and other problems. A good healer removes the blockages and balances the energy.

You must also know what to tell your friend to do at home after his or her healing so that your friend can be involved in the process of healing. Your friend can help keep the energy channels open both physically and spiritually so your friend can stay healthy. This makes your job easier, and your friend will feel better.

Knowing what to do is important, but something else is more important. You must have love, forgiveness and kindness in your heart and soul.

If you want to be a good healer, you must really love people from the bottom of your heart. Spring Forest Qigong is spiritual healing, which is also called energy healing or message healing, or information healing, or signal healing. They are all the same.

When you pass energy to help others, you send out healing signals from your mind to others. These signals travel in your energy.

All the energy you send out will carry all your healing signals, information, and messages. No matter what kind of person you are, you can pretend that you are a good person on the surface, but you cannot hide the nature of your spirit, the nature of your love, forgiveness and kindness towards people. People who receive your energy will automatically, through their system, find out whether your energy is really healing or not.

If you have good, purified, love energy, the healing takes place very effectively and smoothly. If you consider healing as business, not love sharing, your healing result will not be that effective. You must have unconditional love and support for your friend.

Many people have this experience. When you first meet a person, you do not know why you like him or her right away, and later on you find out that he or she is the right person for you. But the one you do not like too much when you first met turns out later on that he or she is not the right person you want to deal with. This feeling becomes even stronger when you are a Qigong practitioner. Because every one has a sixth sense. This sixth sense actually forms a protection to you. So if a healer does not have love energy, the universal love energy in his soul, others will find that out through their sixth sense, and spiritually, people will not accept the healers energy.

That is why we often emphasize that love, forgiveness and kindness are fundamental for all types of energy healing. The level of your healing power depends on the level of love you have toward your friends. It is hard to imagine that a person without love can become a good healer. The more purified your energy is, the more powerful and effective your healing will become. When people come to see me, I consider them as my mother, or father, or brother, or sister, or my own children. I will do anything I can to help them and I will not ask for anything in return. That is unconditional and pure love.

Energy healing is of love sharing. It is a healing from the soul. You don't argue with your friends. Do whatever you are guided to do. If your soul is pure, your love is there, the universe knows how to assist you and it will also reward you in the best possible way!

Techniques are the second most important thing. If you have good will to help others but you do not know how to help them, you are be limited in what you can do to help. Many other healers try to keep the healing techniques to themselves. Sometimes they do not know how to teach someone else to heal – they can do it, but they can't teach others. Also, some of the techniques out there are either too complicated or too difficult to learn. They require a person to spend years to learn and practice before she/he can use them to help others.

Here in Spring Forest Qigong we open the secret of Qigong healing and make it simple for everybody to learn. Actually, healing is very simple, especially for spiritual healing. We all know prayer is healing. Good wishes are healing. Many critical diseases are healed through prayer. My masters always told me and warned me that the most powerful thing in the world is usually the simplest thing in the world.

Please be patient when you are learning Qigong healing. The techniques are simple, but there are many tips I will give you so that you could become a more powerful healer.

Five keys for successful Qigong healing

You may remember these from Level One. They are so important that I want to repeat them here, and tell you how they relate to helping others to heal. If you want to make your healing successful, you need to have:

> *1. Faith*
>
> *2. Confidence*
>
> *3. Master's energy*
>
> *4. Visualization*
>
> *5. Focus*

Let's talk about Faith

Faith is spiritual. Faith does not come from knowledge, but from the soul. Knowledge and experience can help strengthen faith.

Doing energy healing we need to have faith. You do not have to be a religious person but you do need to have faith in a power greater than yourself. If you are a religious person, that is wonderful. It does not matter what religion you belong to, you can choose to believe in God, or Jesus Christ, or to believe in Buddha, or Loazu. You can choose to believe in the universe, or your spiritual master or any spiritual figures you have high respect to, but you must have faith. Faith gives us the spirit and life force to run the physical body.

The stronger your faith, the stronger your healing because you will draw on the energy of your spiritual master to help heal your friends.

In my understanding, these spiritual figures have given us so much guidance in the spiritual healing and have proved what they said. We need to trust them. We should have faith in them. Through my years of experience in healing, I really feel that the more trust I have in them, the more healing power I am given. Having faith in them is also a journey of purifying your energy. When you have more faith in them, you will automatically follow their teaching and do what they have done for others and the world. You will love and help people in the way they do. The more you do as they do, the more you will purify your energy, and the more peace and calmness you will have in your life. The journey of your healing is a journey of trusting. The journey of your healing others is a journey of healing yourself, developing yourself, and purifying yourself, spiritually and physically.

In the Western world many people go to church regularly and they believe all the stories of Jesus, but I really don't know how many people believe what Jesus said about healing, that everybody can do healing as he did. Here in Level Two, I am going to share with you what I have learned and show you that everyone can learn how to send out energy to help others heal, like what Jesus could do. This healing is not Voodoo, but a science of the body, spirit, and the mind that is thousands of years old. It is an ancient science that modern scientists are now studying.

The second key is Confidence

Confidence comes from faith and knowledge. Once you have faith in what you are doing and the knowledge of how to make your healing work, you need to gain confidence to help the healing work better.

How can you increase your confidence? Do more good deeds and healing for others without asking anything in return. The more good things you do for others out of your soul, the more joy will grow within you, and more confidence you will have in helping others.

Each time, when you are helping your friend, you let the universal energy flow through you to pass it to your friend. You become a conduit to direct more healing energy to your friend. Nothing more; nothing less.

Forget yourself. Forget your worry. Forget your reputation. Forget your fame. Surrender yourself totally to the universe. Know that the universe does the healing through you. You are only a tool of the universe for healing your friend and your family. If you think in this way, your worry will go away. Your confidence will grow. Confidence is the key to make your healing more effective. The more confidence you have in your healing, the better result you will get.

Confidence is built up not in one day, but through your consistent practice. It is so common that when you see good result of your healing, you feel so good, and you think you have the energy to heal the world. But next time when your healing is not that successful, you doubt whether you really have the healing power to heal others.

Through more and more practice, you will gain more experience and confidence.

Here I want you to know that, according to my healing experience in the United States, about 15 percent of my clients have an energy system that is extremely sensitive. When I say, without moving my hand to do the healing, your blockages are gone now, they get very excited and feel better right away.

About 35 percent of my clients have an energy system that is very sensitive. By moving the energy around for a while, they will feel better or the blockages are almost gone--I have to do very little work.

About 35 percent are average sensitive. These people need two or more healing sessions before they feel some change.

10 percent are between sensitive and not sensitive. You need

more times with them before they could feel something.

About 5 percent are not sensitive. Even when you put a needle into their bodies, they might say they don't feel anything. For these people I suggest they use medicine, needles, massage and Qigong together, the result would be better.

I also found out that people who are artists, musicians, writers, poets, dancers, singers, priests, psychologists, etc., have energy that is very easy to work with because they have more image thinking. But people who work in the science field such as in chemistry, physics, etc., their spiritual energy system and belief system are sometimes not as open. It is not always easy to work on these people and it requires extra effort because they have more logical thinking.

People who are very kind and forgiving, are so easy to heal. People who are stubborn and aggressive, and who always have negative ideas about people and things, are not that easy to work with. For these people, introduce them to Qigong information and help educate them about the love, forgiveness, and kindness of this universal energy to help them to purify their energy and open their spiritual channels.

Call upon the master's energy.

This is the third key to success in practicing Spring Forest Qigong. Before you do Qigong, self-healing, or helping others to heal, call upon your master's energy.

Energy healing or spiritual healing is a signal healing, informational healing, and message healing. We can pass our energy to help others heal. But as an individual, we do not have sufficient energy to give. We must draw on energy outside of our body such as the universal energy and the energy of our master.

Who is the master?

The master is someone who has very purified energy, who has very good healing energy, and for whom you have very high respect. This is a Chinese concept and some people in the west are confused by this.

The word master has many meanings. A master can be a highly regarded teacher or guide. A master is always someone for whom you have the highest respect.

At the very top, would be a spiritual master. A spiritual master is someone of the highest and most purified spiritual energy, such as Jesus Christ, or Buddha, or Moses or Laotzu.

At the next level, a master could be someone such as a wonderful and loving grandma or grandpa.

Then, would come a teacher, such as, myself. If you like my energy, you can call upon my energy, as well.

Or you can call upon all of these people's energy together. But no matter whose energy you call upon, you must have high respect for them. If you call upon someone's energy that you do not truly respect, you will never get it.

To call on your master's energy is easy. Stretch open your hands. Call upon your master's energy using the intention of your mind. When you feel tingly in your hands, warmness runs throughout your body, or you can see light, color around you, or you can smell something very nice and sweet, that means your master's energy is with you.

At first, you may not have any of the above experiences. Don't be concerned about this. As you practice and learn to calm your mind and relax yourself you will eventually have the experience of your master's energy and the universal energy flowing into you. Just know and trust that the energy is there and is flowing into you whether you sense it right away or not.

The relationship between you and the master is like the relationship between radio and radio station. The radio station is constantly sending out a signal. It might be broadcasting beautiful, soothing music that you would very much enjoy. But, you will not be able to enjoy the music unless you do certain things.

First, of course, you must have your radio turned on. If your radio is off, you won't hear anything. The radio station is broadcasting but you are not ready to receive the signal. Secondly, your radio must be tuned to the right station, the right frequency. Sometimes it can take some fine-tuning on your radio to bring in the signal clearly.

Once you tune to the right frequency and get the signal, the signal goes through the amplifier and then to the speaker. If the quality of the speaker is good enough, the sound could be so loud, so powerful it would make the whole room shake.

Finally, you must be listening. If you are busy talking or working, your enjoyment of the music will be limited. It is still there and you can still hear it but to fully enjoy it you must be still and quiet and relaxed. Then, your enjoyment of the beautiful music will be its fullest.

When you call on your master's energy, you are receiving his or her energy signals. Their signals, their energy have no limitation. You will never deplete your master's energy. Just as you can never deplete the universal energy. The supply is inexhaustible.

Your respect for your master is just like your radio. It is through your respect that your radio is turned on. The higher your respect and trust for your master or masters the more powerfully you will receive their signal, their energy.

If you do not have respect for your master, you will never be able to tune to the right frequency and receive the signal. So when you call upon your master's energy, call upon that master's energy that you highly respect.

You can call upon more than one master's energy. But make sure you call upon those for whom you have high respect.

Of course, when you call upon your master's energy, you must do it for good purpose. Otherwise you will never get it. The universal energy knows what to do for you. For instance, if you call upon your master's energy to help you to heal yourself or heal others, that is great. But, if you call upon your master's energy for something that is selfish or harmful, you will never get it. Your master's energy, the universal energy is pure, to receive it you must be serving a good purpose.

After you call upon your master's energy, trust it. Don't put any doubt into it. Strongly believe that the universal energy will know what should be done. You just go ahead to do what you are supposed to do. Whatever happens will happen. Whatever is not going to happen will not happen. Trust that what is good and best will happen. It always does.

The fourth key is Visualization or Imagination

When you do healing, try to visualize or imagine that something is really happening in your friend. You can use whatever image you pick up at the moment and do it. Anything positive and healing will do.

I recommend, as you learned in Level One, to imagine bolts of energy coming from your fingers when you use Sword Fingers to break up blockages. Imagine this energy causing the blockage to turn to smoke or air. Then you grab this smoke or air with your hands and pull it away. See it in your mind or use your imagination. Then use your palms and imagine energy coming through your palms to heal your friend.

The more vivid your imagination whether you use visual images, sounds, or feelings, the more powerful your healing.

There are other ways to use visualization. Here let me share a story with you so that you know one of the ways I used visualization.

A lady who was diagnosed with breast cancer and lung cancer came to see me. I tried all I knew to help her unblock the blockages but my energy just could not get into her body. I called upon my masters energy again. In a minute I saw in my mind a beautiful rose dancing in front of me. I wondered what it was. Then a message came to me. *Plant the rose*. I visualized myself taking hold of the rose and planting it into that lady's chest. Part of the root went into the lung where she had the blockage and part of the root went into her blocked breast. I visualized all the blockages change into wonderful fertilizer and help the rose grow. The rose was growing bigger and bigger and looked so beautiful and no more fertilizer left in the body. Then I talked to the rose. "Hey rose, it is not a good place for you to live forever. Let me move you to a forest and plant you by the river." So I did.

The next morning my friend came back to see me. Right at the moment she got into my place, she cried. I asked her why she cried. She said that that morning when she took a shower before she came to see me, she found the tumor in the breast disappeared! Then she told me the other part of the story. After she saw me the day before, she went to do some shopping. When she got home, before she opened the door, she smelled roses around her. She looked around her on the snow, but found nothing. She opened the door; the rose smell was still there. She looked around the house. She assumed that her husband might have bought some flowers for her. But she found no flowers in the house. When she put her groceries down, she found some rose smell coming out from her chest. She felt very strange.

I told her what I did the last day. A few months later, she called me and told me that the doctor could not find the tumor in her lung either.

I have many healing stories like this. Let me tell you two more stories so you see how powerful visualization is.

A musician came to see me. He had depression and a shoulder problem. But what bothered him most was that whenever he composed music, his hand would lose control, and then his mind would lose control, too. His hand kept moving until he finished the music. When he woke up and looked at the music, he would not recognize the music was written by him. Then he would get very frightened and upset. He punched glass windows and cut himself on the glass. This happened to him many times. It was very dangerous. He had been to many psychologists. But he was not helped.

When I first met him, he was really down. He had no energy to talk. His two friends came along to help him explain what happened to him.

When I detected the blockages. I found huge blockages in his heart and head. I worked on him. I visualized some birds were living in his heart and head. I talked to the birds that they should find a better place than the head and the heart to live. Then I visualized the birds flying out of the heart and head and going back to the universe. I felt so grateful to them. I could see them very happy, going back to the universe. Since then he was healed.

Another person had arthritis in the whole spine. She said the whole spine was painful and cold. I visualized a big long silver snake in the spine. I kept pulling the snake out of the spine, a long one, and put the snake back to a mountain. After I was done with my work, she said that she felt something moving out of the spine and disappeared. I worked on her a couple more times and then her spine problems were completely gone.

I tell you these stories to encourage and inspire you. There are many ways to do good healing. The possibilities are endless when you use your imagination.

Now, let's continue with the fifth key, Focus

When you do meditation, you need to focus on the good feeling in the body but not your symptoms. When you do healing, you need to relax yourself and focus on how fast your friends symptoms disappear. When you detect the blockages, you can try to find the blockages in the body so that you know what part of the body you need to work on. But after you find out the blockage, when you do healing, you do not focus on the blockages any more. You focus on how fast the blockages open, how powerful the healing energy is, like a current in the ocean, like the heat in a volcano, like a stampede of wild horses. etc.

When you focus, you do not need to focus on that area for a long time. A few seconds or a couple minutes will do. Doing healing, it does not matter how long you can focus on the blockage, but how fast and strong you send energy over to break the blockages. This is why people who receive my healing could feel the result so fast. You want to get the pain away in one minute, not in one week! Of course, when you do healing, you need to draw energy from the universe and store it in your lower Dantian or middle Dantian before you send the energy out to help others. In this way, you have more energy and gain more energy than what you spend. I recommend the middle Dantian more because it is more powerful and it helps you to open channels faster. Your middle Dantian is located under the bottom of your heart.

Energy Systems of the Body and Color Healing

The body has different energy systems that involve multiple organs. A blockage in one organ often indicates blockages in other organs within its energy system.

Knowing the relationship among the organs is very helpful in our healing. Each energy system responds favorably to various colors which can increase the healing. When giving energy through the palm(s) to the heart system, for example, imagine red or pink energy. Staring at colored paper or a colored light can enhance your visualization of that color because your eyes are left with signals from that color.

The Liver System

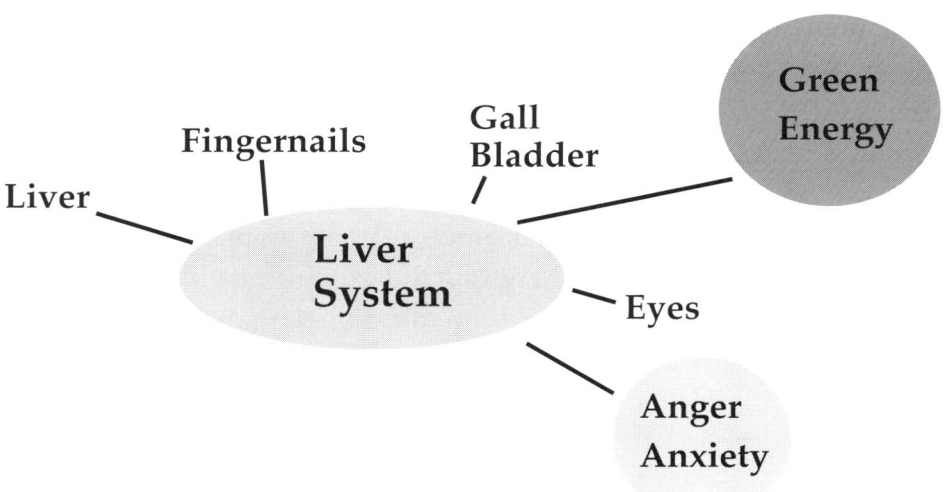

The Kidney System

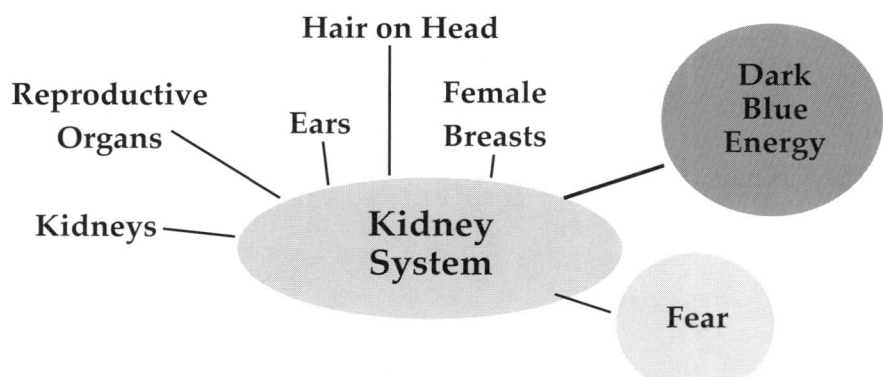

Kidney energy is the life force energy and affects our overall strength and stamina. Low kidney energy is associated with weight gain, loss of hearing, and so on.

The Stomach System

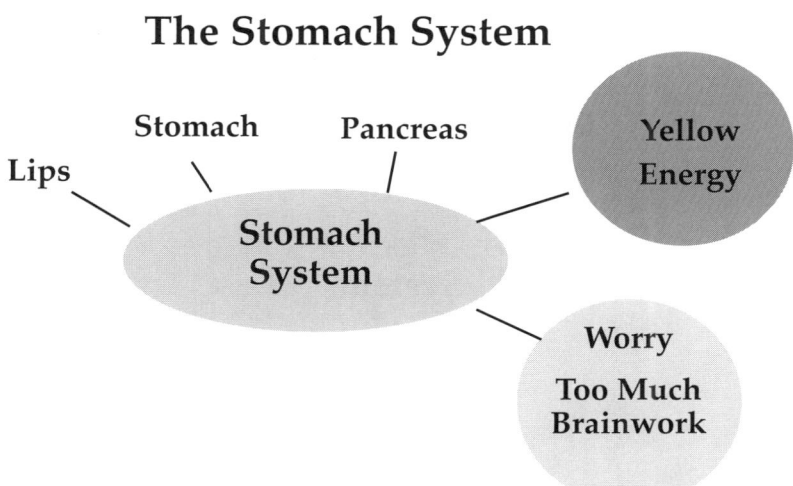

The Breathing System

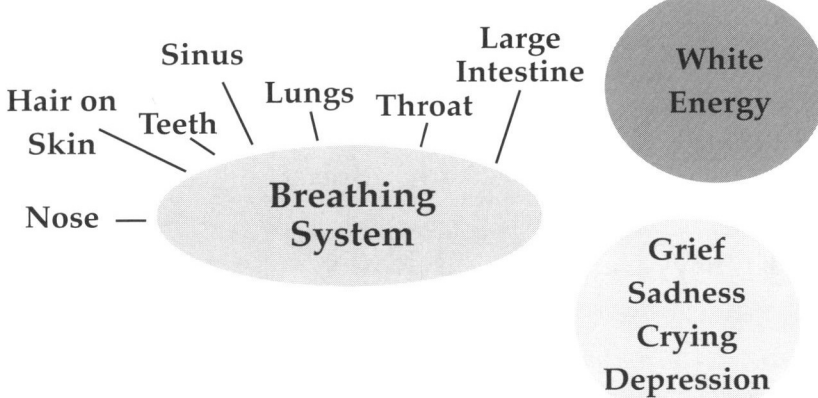

Blockages in one organ can cause problems in the others. A person with digestive problems might also have a stuffy head and skin problems.

The Heart System

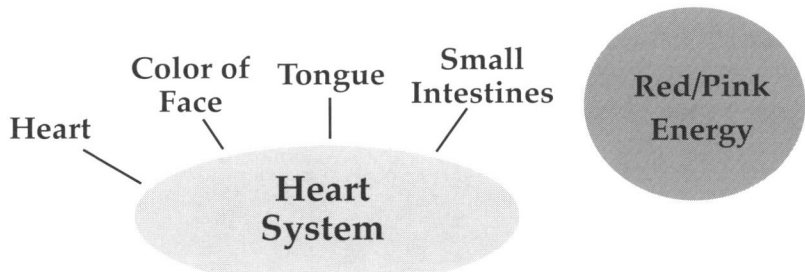

Over excitement, such as extremes of happiness or unhappiness adversely affects this system.

General Healing Technique

Thousands of Spring Forest Qigong students have already used the following techniques to help heal their friends.

Now, let's get into the good stuff. This is how I do healing for other people. Let's begin with my three secrets that can help you with your Qigong Healing. These are the same three secrets we discussed in Level One. They are important whether you want to heal yourself or help heal your friend.

1) *Go into the emptiness to connect with the universe.*

When go into the emptiness while you are doing healing, you can purify your energy better and make your healing more effective and powerful. In the emptiness, you forget your entire burden in your everyday life so that you can focus better on helping others. Begin by saying the password to yourself:

> "I am in the universe.
> The universe is in my body.
> The universe and I combine together."

2) *Stay simple.*

Healing is not complicated. Do not make it complicated by adding rituals or other techniques. Keep your healing process simple to help your healing energy flow smoothly. Not everyone can be a rocket scientist, but almost anyone can be a healer. That's how simple it is. Remember, the most powerful thing usually is the simplest thing, especially when you do spiritual healing.

3) *Use your consciousness*

The way you are thinking, the attitude you have to healing, the message you send out to the body of your friend, and the confidence level while you are doing your healing are all important. So always be positive about your healing. Get rid of your doubt.

Trust the universal energy. It will move through you to help heal your friend. Trust your master's energy.

Qigong healing is message healing, signal healing and information healing. It relies on intention and focus. The message you send is energy. You send your best wishes for your friend to help them heal.

The secrets to make your healing successful.
The Importance of Confidence in Healing

Confidence is also a key factor in healing. The more confidence you have the more successful you can be.

We are all one; the atom and the solar system are built from the same model, just to a different scale. The healing work is done by the universal energy that flows through us, not by the motions we go through. But the motions can help conduct the flow of the healing energy.

When we do healing, we let our body become an empty vessel. Let the universal energy, or spiritual energy, or God's energy, or Jesus' energy, or Buddha's energy, or Laozu's energy, or whatever purified and beautiful healing energy flow into our body and then pass it into your friend's body and help him to heal. In this way while we are helping to heal others, we get ourselves healed at the same time. So we can use the techniques to help heal others and to also heal ourselves.

Some people who believe in Jesus Christ have told me that only Jesus can heal. I say to them that it is Christ's healing energy that flows through you to help heal your friend. You do not actually heal your friend. You merely use your body and your mind to help Christ's energy. The more purified you are, the more energy will be flowing through you to make your healing energy more powerful.

No matter your spiritual beliefs, you do not heal. The energy heals. You must be humble and grateful that you can use your body to help conduct the flow of healing energy.

As a matter of fact, every time you finish a healing session with a friend, thank him for giving you the opportunity to help.

We connect with the universal energy by going into the emptiness (secret 1); we then use our consciousness to direct the energy into healing (secret 3). The energy flows most strongly when we keep it simple (secret 2). Our doubts about our ability to heal others and ourselves adds complexity. The more confident we are, the quicker and more powerful our healing will be. While technique is important, confidence makes the technique better.

The very amazing thing of Qigong healing is that you don't necessarily need to know the locations of different organs before you can do your healing. Somehow healing energy will always find where it needs to go within the body. For instance, if you want to help a person with liver blockages, don't know where the liver is, and you pass energy into the throat, once the energy gets into the throat, it knows where to go! The only thing you need to do is to say in your mind, "The liver channels open. Completely healed!" And you repeat this message while you are doing the healing. It is very safe. We will never do any harm to the body.

You don't need to know the body, just know how to give energy. If you know the locations of the organs, it helps to conduct the healing energy better.

One more very important point. This energy can only heal, it can never do harm.

Some people wonder what might happen if someone wants to use this technique to do bad things to other people. The universe will stop it, and this person will gradually lose the ability to do spiritual energy healing work. To use this energy, you must have love in your heart. It will not work if you do not have love.

The Healing Process: Step by Step

The most important consideration in all healing situations, whether you are healing yourself or others, is that it must be done from an attitude of love, forgiveness, and kindness. Technique is definitely secondary to attitude.

Below is an outline of the steps of Qigong Healing. Following the outline, I go into the steps in more detail. You will find even more detail on the pages that follow. Review this section carefully and often to ensure you do the best healing possible.

Opening
- Prepare your friend
- Prepare yourself
- Detect blockages
- Small Universe (3 times)
- Lower Dantian (9 times)

Healing (repeat as necessary)
- Open spine at C7
- Open other areas of spine
- Break up blockages
- Pull out blocked energy
- Give energy

Closing
- Small Universe (3 times)
- Lower Dantian (9 times)
- Bring your friend "back"
- Give positive message
- Thank your friend

Now let's go into more detail.

Opening

Prepare your friend.

Have your friend seat herself/himself comfortably. If your friend knows nothing about energy healing explain that he needs only to close his eyes, breathe comfortably, and relax. Explain that you will begin by detecting blockages, then you will move energy to clear the blockages and return new energy to the area where you remove blockages. Ask if you may do so. The key to a healer's success is trust. Promise nothing—healers only help others to heal themselves.

If your friend has high blood pressure, headache, or fever, please ask him to put his hands facing down on the lap. For low blood pressure, ask him to put his hands facing up. (Putting the hands facing up and down assists the proper flow of the energy in his body.) Otherwise, your friend might simply put the hands up like holding a ball in front, or rest his hands on his lap with his hands facing up.

It is not necessary to have your friend put his tongue against the roof of the mouth unless he knows Qigong or practices Qigong. It may otherwise make him nervous. When he is not relaxed, it is not easy to remove the blockages from his body.

Before you pass energy to do your healing, relax yourself.

Take a deep breath three times. Talk in your mind, 'All my channels open. I have no energy blockage in the body. All my blockages, pain (whatever) are gone. I am completely healed.' Then relax yourself as if you are taking a nap." In this way you help your friend to become very calm and more fully relaxed.

If you plan to do half an hour healing, you can play the recorded session from Level One, Self-Concentration or one of my music CDs. The music can help your friend become calm and relaxed faster and go deeper into the meditation.

Prepare yourself.

Rub your hands together. Connect with the universal energy and your own energy. Connect with your master's energy and any other energy that is helpful to you or your friend. Once you have the master's energy, the universal energy with you, you will have tremendous energy to use. You will not deplete your own energy.

Hold a loving, positive attitude. Fear or doubt can infect you and the other person if you allow it to intrude. Remember that healers do not perform healing, they only help others heal themselves.

Detecting blockages.

Perform the detection technique described on page 47-48. Most importantly, trust yourself. During the process of detecting, you will be moving through and interacting with your friend's Qi. Work from top to bottom and not vice versa. (Working bottom-up can disrupt the flow of Qi in especially sensitive or sick people with high blood pressure, heart problems, fever, or headaches when you do it this way for a long period of time.)

Small Universe.

Perform the steps of Small Universe, described on page 45-46.

Lower Dantian

Give energy to your friend's lower Dantian nine times.

Healing

Follow these steps for each blockage. You will find additional information for specific problems and areas of the body later in this course manual.

Open spine at C7

Point Sword Fingers to the C7 area of the spine, which is where the neck meets the upper back at the shoulders. Move Sword Fingers around to break up the blockages with energy that flows from your Sword Fingers.

Open other areas of spine

Use Sword Fingers to open the areas of the spine associated with the detected blockages.

Use Sword Fingers to break up the blockage.

Visualize the Sword Finger energy changing blockages into "air" or "smoke." (Exception: never use Sword Fingers on the heart from front. The heart rejects Sword Finger energy.)

Pull out the excess, blocked energy.

Use your hands, fingers open to pull or sweep energy away from blocked areas. Imagine taking hold of the "air" or "smoke" and releasing this extra energy to the earth or universe. Keep pulling the "air" or "smoke" out and releasing the energy to the universe until you feel the blockage is clear—you want to feel emptiness in your hands. Keep your hands open—do not make a fist. With body parts that come in pairs (such as arms, legs, eyes, kidneys, and lungs) clear and unblock both, beginning with the clear or less-blocked one. (Exceptions: never pull energy directly out of the top of the head or from the front of the heart. If you do that for a long period of time you might help the body lose energy that the body needs.)

Give Energy

Put energy into the area you are working on using your palm(s) by gently moving your hand(s) in and out nine times, as discussed in Level One. This can be done either now, before clearing the blocked energy, or afterward. (Exceptions: do not put energy into the head before you remove the blockage for a headache; and do not give energy to the tooth for a toothache, because this is not helpful.)

Say to yourself with great confidence, "Blockages open. Pains are completely gone. You are completely healed."

Closing

Repeat Small Universe three times

This will help make sure the back channel and the front channel stay open.

Give energy to your friend's lower Dantian nine times

You will help the person heal faster and prolong the healing results.

Bring your friend back from the meditation.

Ask her to open her eyes and take three deep breaths. Ask her to rub hands together. Ask her to massage her face.

Give a positive closing message, such as "Feel better now?"

We use a positive message to replace the old message in your friend's brain. People have told me that they still felt pain until I asked them how wonderful they felt—the pain totally went away.

Thank your friend in your heart for allowing you to help him/her.

It is not necessary to say it out loud. It is what you feel in your heart that is more important.

Thank the Universe and your master, in your heart, for giving you such a great opportunity to share your love and energy with others and for giving you the energy to do so.

Small Universe

Open the Small Universe to open and connect the front and back energy channels in your friend.

You will use your hands to move energy along the front and back of the body in fluid movements. The process is demonstrated on the video.

1) Stand on the left side of your friend, who is seated. If necessary, you may stand on the right side and your friend may lie down.

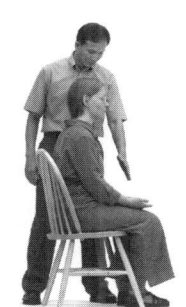

2) Use your left hand to send energy into your friend's lower Dantian nine times. If you stand on the right side, use your right hand to send energy.

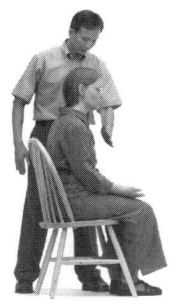

3) Move your left hand down to the bottom of the torso, passing energy through your palm.

4) Move your left hand away and put it to your left side.

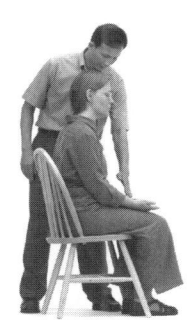

5) Then use your right hand (palm facing your friend about six to nine inches away) to move energy up the back of the torso.

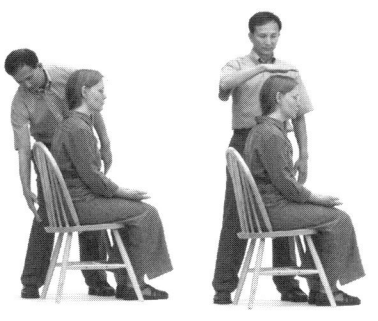

6) You will move your hand from the tailbone level to the top of her head. Stop with your hand over her head.

7) Then move your left hand up from the bottom of your torso to about throat level, then placing your left hand (palm down) over her head (over your right hand).

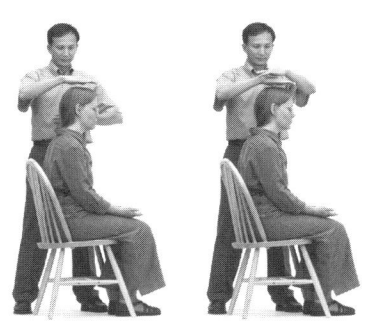

8) Move your right hand down your torso with your palm facing your torso and put it on your right side.

9) Move energy down your friend's front torso with your left hand, palm toward her.

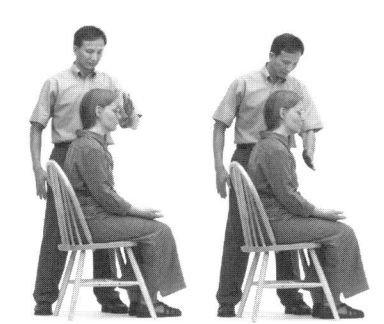

10) Then repeat. These motions produce two, fluid, intersecting loops. They are generally repeated three times, or until you feel "done."

11) When you feel you are done with this motion, your left hand stops over the lower Dantian. Give energy into the lower Dantian nine times.

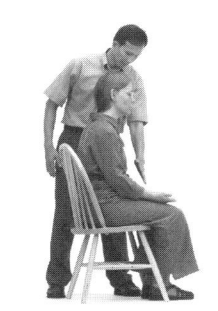

Detecting Blockages

"Blockages" refer to places in our physical and energetic body where the energy does not flow smoothly.

The smooth, balanced flow of energy (chi or Qi) is critical to robust physical health. When our channels become blocked, Qi may accumulate in one place and be depleted in another (like water forms a lake behind a dam and leaves the stream below it nearly dry).

Blockages may be located in a different area or areas of the body from where the pain or symptoms are felt. For example, your friend may have pain in the temple area of the head while the energy blockage is in the neck.

To heal your friend, find the root of the sickness, which is the blockage. Do not focus on the symptoms.

Most people can detect blockages with their hands, as demonstrated on the video. Your hand may shake or tingle or itch, or your hand may feel changes in temperature or degrees of wetness and dryness. For most people, the more intense the reaction, the stronger the blockage.

There are also other ways to feel blockages. You may feel other people's blockages in your own body as pressure, pain, twinges, etc. You may also receive messages through thoughts or feelings. Honor all these paths—they are all ways to do detection.

To detect blockages, pose clear, unambiguous questions to the universe, such as: Is there a blockage on the top of the head? the side of the head? by the eyes? the nose? the mouth? the throat? in the lungs? the heart? On the surface, middle, or back of the organ? etc. Too general of questions, such as "Is there anything going on here?" will produce ambiguous results.

You may also detect temperature information—this is not body heat that you might detect with your hand, but rather energetic temperature. The heart energy should feel warm; the lungs should feel cool and you may feel a tingle; the liver and kidneys should feel cool to warm or tingly, but not hot or cold. With the other parts of the body the feeling should be even. If you find the energy in an area too warm it indicates too much Yang energy. If the energy is too cold it indicates too much Yin energy.

Keep your shoulders relaxed and your attention on your friend's body (not your hand). Slowly move your hand from side to side to scan your friend's body. (I prefer to use one hand instead of two, because the feeling of one hand is different from the other. If you use both your hands to detect the blockage, you may be confused.)

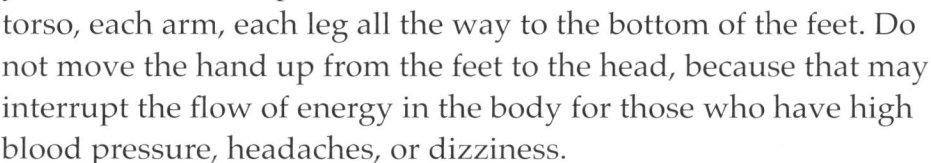

Hold your hand ten inches or more from your friend's physical body (far enough so that you are not detecting her physical body heat). Move your hands from top to bottom, down her head, torso, each arm, each leg all the way to the bottom of the feet. Do not move the hand up from the feet to the head, because that may interrupt the flow of energy in the body for those who have high blood pressure, headaches, or dizziness.

When you feel something abnormal in your hand, you have found a blockage. Trust what you detect. You do not have to repeat the process - you do not have to double check.

A blockage does not necessarily mean a physical illness in the body. Until a blockage, which starts as Yin energy, changes to Yang, a person cannot feel the blockage. Yang energy often manifests as symptoms.

Clear the Spine First

Begin each healing by clearing the C7 vertebra, which is the seventh vertebra down. It is the bump you can feel on your spine.

Then for all blockages in the body, clear the corresponding area on the spine with Sword Fingers before working on the area with the blockage.

1) When there is a blockage in any internal organ, first use Sword Fingers to open the C7 vertebra in the neck.

2) When you find blockages in the head and shoulders, use Sword Fingers to open the relative part of the neck spine again before you go to the organ

3) When you find blockages in the upper torso, first use Sword Fingers to open the upper part of the spine in the back.

4) Blockages in the middle section of the torso including the stomach, liver, and kidneys have something to do with the lower part of the spine.

5) Blockages in the lower abdomen have something to do with the lower back spine and the tailbone. These blockages include blockages in the bladder and reproductive organs.

6) Blockages in the arms and hands have something to do with the upper spine.

7) Blockages in the legs have something to do in the lower spine.

Special Healing Techniques

The general healing technique that I described earlier applies in most circumstances. However, there are instances when special directions are necessary, or when additional information is helpful in healing

After you open the small universe, you are ready to do specific healing if necessary. Here are some general rules to follow:

- As I said earlier, no matter what internal organ blockages a person has, the first point you should help him open is the #C7 vertebra in the neck.

- Always open the relative part of the spine with your sword fingers before working on the organ.

- This is because any blockages in the upper part of the torso have something to do with the upper part of the spine in the back.

- Any blockages in the middle section including the liver, kidney, and stomach have something to do with the lower part of the spine.

- Any blockages in the lower abdomen have something to do with the lower back spine and the tailbone. These blockages include blockages in the bladder and reproductive organs. Blockages in the arms and hands have something to do with the upper spine, while blockages in the legs have something to do with the lower spine.

Always remember that in Spring Forest Qigong healing, we regard any sickness in the body as extra energy in the body. Our job is to return this extra energy back to the universe. So don't regard the sickness as bad energy. If you put the "bad energy" out there in the earth or the universe, you could poison the land or the universe through your mind. Actually, energy is energy. There is no good or bad energy, until you put it in the right position or wrong position. And don't put this extra energy into your own body either, the message is not good for your health. Here I have a story to share with you.

When I came back to America this time, I met a person who was diagnosed with lung cancer. He had a sweet wife and lovely son. The boy was six years old. I felt so sad for the family. He was doing much better after my first several healings, then he went to see his doctor. His doctor said that he had a type of very aggressive cancer which was impossible to heal. Though at the moment he felt better and there was no growth of the cancer, he will eventually die. He got so frightened that he felt very sick right after that. Then he came to see me again. I felt so sympathetic with him. Then in my healing, I said to the universe, "Let me take his cancer and set him free." Then I visualized his cancer moved to my body and he was healed. Eventually, he passed away because the cancer spread very fast in the body. But that day right after my healing, after I got home, I felt great chest pain in my lungs. It took me several weeks to get rid of the pain. I learned a big lesson.

Now we are going to discuss healing in different parts of the body beginning with the head and working down the body.

Problems in the head (such as headache, ear infection, eye problems, etc.)

You should use your sword fingers to open these four areas---#C7, the base of the head, the top of the head, and the forehead between the two eyebrows before you work those problems. If your friend has a headache, then you will use sword fingers to work on the area where your friend feels pain or discomfort. Then open your hands and visualize your energy fingers going into the area, taking hold of the blockage as smoke, pulling the smoke out, and throwing it to the ends of the universe. Keep doing this until you see no more smoke in your imagination or until the sensation in your hands change.

When you pull the blockage out, do not close your fingers like holding a fist. Hold an empty hand. Try to feel the energy in your hands. Usually at the beginning of your pulling, you could feel a stickiness sensation in your hands. Then the stickiness feeling is getting less and less as you keep pulling . When you do not feel the stickiness sensation any more, the blockage is clear.

Here is an important tip to get your consciousness involved in the healing. At the same time you are pulling out excess energy, say in your mind strongly "THE PAIN IS GONE. YOU ARE COMPLETELY HEALED!" keep repeating this message all the time while you are doing the healing. I'll give you more examples of this later.

When you feel the blockage is clear, you stop, and believe, without any doubt that the blockage is clear! Then you use your palm to give energy back to the area where you pull the blockage out to help enhance the circulation, so that the body can heal faster.

Many other healing techniques that people use to help others just focus on pulling the blockage out of the body without giving healing energy back to the body to help heal. Here we pay great attention to this. While we pull energy out from the body, at the same time, we give a lot of energy back to the body, so that the healing takes place very smoothly in the body.

Here are two important points regarding blockages in the head:

1) Do not pull blockage out directly from the top of the head. As we know, seventy percent of the heat coming out from the body is from the top of the head. If we open the channel in the top of the heat, energy comes out even faster. This is not helpful. So you remove the blockages out from the sides of the head instead of from the top of the head.

2) Do not put energy into the head before you remove blockages out from the head when a person has headache. The channels running through the head at #C7 and the forehead are narrow. Once the energy gets into the head, it is not easy to get it out. When too much energy stays in the head and does not move, problems can develop. If you put more energy into the head without opening the channels first, this is not helpful.

Let's move on to other problems in the head.

Eye Problems

If your friend has eye problems, besides opening the four points in the head, you should open two more points. These points are between the two eyes on both sides of the bridge of the nose. Remove the blockages. Then go to the eyes to open blockages in the eyes.

Work on the eye that has the least blockage first. Whenever a body part comes in pairs, always work on the good part first.

This is true for the ears, lungs, arms, kidneys--everything that comes in pairs.

When you know your friend is nearsighted remove the blockage out from the sides of the eyes. Do not pull directly from the front because the pupil becomes oval for people with nearsightedness.

There is a special technique to remove blockages from the sides of the eye, which I demonstrate on the video. Basically, you remove the blockages by moving one hand up and the other hand down. Or you might just simply use your sword fingers to point to the eyes and move them clockwise in a circular way, visualizing the eyes as round as the full moon.

When you know your friend is far-sighted you can pull from the front, because, the focus of the eye goes deeper in the eyes.

If a person has both nearsighted and far-sighted problems, you use the two techniques together.

The message you use to help with eye problems: *"ALL THE BLOCKAGES ARE GONE. THE FUNCTION OF THE EYES ARE COMPLETELY BACK TO NORMAL."* Of course you don't forget to give energy back to the areas where you remove blockages out.

You can give some exercises for these people to do after your healing. Ask them to do the neck exercise from level one. They can also use the cupped-hand to pat the base of the head with their neck bent forward for two minutes. Then they can rub their hands until they are very hot and use the palms to cover the eyes for two minutes--do this three times. While they are doing so, ask them to repeat in their mind the message: *"MY EYESIGHT IS BACK TO NORMAL. I AM COMPLETELY HEALED. "* These exercises can help keep the channels open for the eyes. Do these exercises three times a day. Of course, the more the better.

If the eyesight is getting weak, or the eyes are itching, watering, they all have something to do with the liver. Do you remember that the eyes are part of the liver energetic system? You need to do the liver first before you treat the eyes. We will discuss how to help with liver problems later.

When your friend has cross-eye problem or cataracts work on the same areas as other eye problems, but pay more attention to the neck, the base of the head, and the two points on the two sides of the bridge of the nose between the eyes.

One good example is worth one thousand words!

Ear Problems

Let's go to ear problems. Remember to first open the four points in the head, which are the C7, base of the head, top of the head, and forehead.

When your friend has an ear infection, use sword fingers on the fleshy part just in front of the ears.

When a person has ear infection in the right ear, you work on the left ear, the good one first. Remember what we have discussed before, energy healing is information healing, signal healing, and message healing. We use the right and healthy messages to correct the wrong message in the body. We wake up the internal energy in the body to help the body heal. When you work on the good one, you are sending messages to the bad one "Hey, right ear, you are not doing the right thing. But the left one is. Here is an example for you to follow." The same thing would happen to other parts of the body too. For instance, when you have a bad shoulder, you focus and massage the good one for ten minutes, and keep repeating "the shoulder pain is gone. Completely heal." After ten minutes or so you try your bad shoulder and see what happens. Your bad shoulder is much better. People asked me in the class what if both shoulders hurt? I asked them to find an area where it did not hurt and massage that part of their shoulders. Get the message to the shoulders and correct the wrong information there.

I learned this simple but powerful technique from my son.

When my son was little, like all the little kids at the same age, he did not behave well at the table. I said it again and again that he should not play with his food on the table, but he did not understand why I said so. Sometimes I had to use father's power to stop him.

One day, his cousin came to play with him and she stayed for dinner. As usual, Ming, my son played with his food again. I looked at him and said, "Ming, look at how well your cousin is eating. See how much food you litter in front on your table." He looked at his table and looked over to his cousin's. He quickly picked up the food on the table and placed it in his bowl. Since then, he very seldom played with food any more.

Hearing Problems

When your friend has hearing loss, ringing in the ears (if this is not caused by the damage of working environment), or water flowing in the ears, look to the kidneys for blockages, because the ears are part of the kidney system. When the kidney energy is weak, hearing is weak. A good sign that your kidney energy is weak is when you begin noticing hearing problems. This is a signal for you to take care of your body now. So you need to clear blockages in the kidneys. Strengthen the kidney energy through those exercises you learn in Level One. Get plenty of sleep.

When your friend is deaf in one or both ears, work on the kidneys, of course, but focus more on the base of the head. When deafness is caused by wrong medication or fever, you can do the same. If there is nerve damage, however, it is difficult to repair the nerves using the techniques in this Level. More advanced work is necessary.

For deaf ears, the last thing you need to do is to use your middle fingers to press the front part of the ears in and shut down the air flowing into the ears. Hold in this position for about five minutes. And then all of a sudden move your fingers away. If at the moment you move your fingers away the person hears the sound "Pong", the channels will be 80% open and the hearing ability comes back. While you are holding your fingers, you repeat in your mind, *"THE HEARING ABILITY COMES BACK. COMPLETELY HEALED!"*

Nose or Throat Problems

When your friend has nose or throat problems, whether sinus problems, a stuffy nose, bloody nose, or sore or dry throat, you must also work on the lungs, because the nose is part of the breathing system. Of course, do the four points in the head first, then the lungs, and then the nose or throat. For nose problems, focus on the base of the head and the forehead. For bloody nose problems, look to the gallbladder and pancreas for blockages.

Teeth and Jaw Related Problems

When your friend has teeth problems open the regular points, you use sword fingers to open all the teeth channels in circular motions around closed mouth, remove blockages out, and put energy in.

But for a toothache, do not put energy in. The palm's energy belongs to Yang energy while the energy in the teeth belongs to Yin. The Yang energy will not help a toothache. This is the only case that I do not put energy in after my healing.

For any other teeth related problems, you deal with the same procedures as you deal with other problems. This is, detect the blockage, remove it, and give healing energy.

Once I helped a high school student with his teeth. He fell and hit his front teeth when he played basketball. The doctor said that the two front teeth were damaged and the nerve there was dead. He suggested removing the teeth. His mother brought him to me. Two times seeing him, he went back to see the doctor. To his surprise, the nerve in the teeth became alive again.

When your friend has TMJ problems, look for the blockage in the neck and the base of the head. So open the neck first, and then the base of the head. And then you open the areas in front of the ears where the joints of the jaw meet. Remove blockages out and put energy in. That is all. The message you use is *"ALL THE JOINTS OPEN. COMPLETELY HEALED!"*

Facial Pain and other Head Problems

When your friend has facial pain or other problems in the head, do the four main points first, then go to the problem area to use sword fingers to break the sick magnetic field. Clear the blockage out and put energy in, and repeat to yourself, *"PAIN IS GONE. COMPLETELY HEALED!"*

Shoulder and Neck Problems

When your friend has Shoulder or neck pain or tightness, look to an energy imbalance in the pancreas unless the problem comes from an injury. When the pancreas is congested, the energy piles up in the shoulders and does not flow freely. This causes tightness and the pain. Clear the pancreas first, and then clear blockages from the neck and shoulders.

When you do the shoulders, you do the good one first. As we have already explained before, energy healing is information healing, signal healing and message healing. Once you get the right message into the body, the body will help you to find the right kind of energy to heal the pain. So you do the good one first. By doing so you set up a good example for the "bad guy" to follow.

Healing any part of the body follows the same philosophy. Healing the kidneys, healing the knees, healing the lungs, healing the arms, etc., you do the good side first before you come to the bad one. In this way, you wake up that person's system to help you. You spend less time and energy but get better result.

Let's continue moving down the body to the lungs.

When we say lung problems, we mean all the energy problems in the breathing system including problems with the nose, throat, large intestine, and hair on the skin, and the skin.

As we know, lung's energy is very important in the body. When we breath in, part of the energy goes to the kidneys, part of the energy goes to help digest the food we eat, and the other part of the energy goes to help purify the blood. So when a person has problems in the large intestines, work on the lungs first. When a person has problems in the skin, work on the lungs first.

Here are the procedures to do the lung healing on your friend:

After opening the #C7 vertebra, you go to the relative part of the spine in the back Then you go to the front to open the areas under the collar bones, which I call the windows of the lungs. I think all of us notice this----when we have coughing, the first place we pat the body to release the tightness is the upper chest or the area under the collarbones. It is just like when there is some smoke in a room; we go to open the doors and windows to let out the smoke. But nobody would go to open the closets. So open the windows first!

After opening these areas, you go to the lungs. No matter what blockages, either in one lung or two lungs, you need to do both lungs because they work together in the breathing system. When one side of the lungs goes wrong, the other side more or less would have some problem too. The way you clear blockages out from the lungs, after you break out the sick magnetic field, is like this----you either stand in front or the back of the person, open your two hands, move the hands down from the shoulders to the bottom of the lungs. At the same time clear the blockages from outside of the lungs to the inner part of the lungs. Repeat this many times until you feel the blockages are clear. Then you give energy back to the lungs to help heal the lungs faster. I demonstrate this technique for you on the video; it is easy to do once you see me do it.

Do you remember which color to visualize the energy to be when doing healing on the lungs? White. Pure, bright white. Let it radiate through your lungs.

After your healing, you can show your friend some exercise to do. You can ask him to hold his arms up above the head with fingers open for ten minutes or more, three or more times a day. Or you can show him/her one of those movements you learned in Level One. This will help heal faster and keep the channels open.

I had a friend who was caught in the big mountain fire in California many years ago. Her lungs were filled with ash. The hospital could not do anything for her and later on, it developed into Asthma. She coughed a lot, could hardly breathe. When she came to see me, she could hardly finish a short sentence and she looked very weak and depressed. When she described what happened to her she cried.

I worked on her three times. She felt she could breathe naturally. The cough stopped. She went to take an x-ray, the lungs were cleared and the ash disappeared!

How could ash disappear? Because, as you learned in Level One, Energy is Energy. It can not be created. Neither can it be destroyed, but it can be transformed, from one form to another.

Ash is a form of energy. It can also be transformed, through a certain technique. We all know that food we put into our stomach can be transformed into many different kinds of energy and go to different parts of the body through the digestive system, through chemical activities. Through the chemical activities, we can also change the ash into smoke to come out of the body or change it into another kind of energy and have it come out through the immune system and Qi system. It is possible to transform the energy of any sickness.

Let's move on to healing heart problems.

Heart is the place where our soul lives. You can use sword fingers to open energy blockages from the back for heart problems, but do not do so from the front of the torso to the heart. The vibration of the energy from the sword fingers does not agree to that of the heart. The quality of sword finger's energy is more negative while the heart's energy is more positive. I think we all notice this. When you greet somebody, or when you introduce someone to others, you very seldom see people use one finger or sword fingers to point to each other. If someone points to you with sword fingers when you are introduced to others, you feel very uncomfortable. This is not the type of energy to give people a warm feeling. So you need to be careful when you use sword fingers on heart problems. Sword fingers won't hurt the heart, but they won't help the heart either.

Helping people with heart problems is one of the strongest areas in my healing. I found these four tips are very useful in the healing:

1) Wear a smile on your face. When you do healing on other parts of the body, you can wear a serious look on your face. But doing healing on the heart, you must wear a smile on your face, and this smile must come from your heart. Once you smile, the quality of the healing energy will totally change. It becomes more healing, and the soul of your friend can feel your healing energy right away and open a door for you to come in to help him.

2) Give energy to the heart first before you remove energy blockage out from the heart.

3) While you remove energy out from the heart, keep giving energy back into the heart frequently. The heart likes that. Remember to visualize red or pink energy.

4) You break energy blockages from the back. And you can remove blockages out from either the front or the back. When you remove blockages, you move your hands in a heart-shaped movement around the heart. Clear in this manner, working from the outer layers of the heart to the inner layers of the heart.

After your healing, you can ask your friend to massage the sides of his middle and little fingers three times a day for ten minutes. Noon is a good time to do heart healing as well as this massage, because at noon the heart channels open and the healing will be more complete. Other Level One exercises such as "Moving of Yin and Yang", "Joining of Yin and Yang" are also good for heart problems. Here's another tip: if your friend has warts on the toes and the fingers, clear blockages from the heart first before you come to the fingers or the toes.

Let's move on to liver problems.

As we know, 70% of the toxins in the body comes out through the liver. In China, when children or someone else in the family get a tumor in the neck or under arm, etc., grandma would go to get something to make some soup to cool down the liver and take care of the heat in the liver. Often by doing so, the tumor would go away.

When doing healing on the liver, open #C7, and then the part of the spine relative to the liver. And then do the liver. The procedures of doing the liver are the same as you do on other problems. But, for the liver visualize green energy when you give energy to the liver.

When you work on the liver, you need to work on the gall bladder, too. When the liver has extra energy, the energy goes to the gallbladder and changes into the bile, which is used to help digest food. So when a person has digesting problems, the first place you need to focus is the liver and the gallbladder. In other words, if a person's liver is good, his digestion is also good.

Pancreas works closely with the liver. So you need to balance the energy in the pancreas while you do healing to the liver, and vice versa.

Liver's energy shows out through the eyes. When a person's vision is not doing well, or when the eyes cannot see as well as before, you need to work on the liver. The liver's energy might be weak or there are some blockages in the liver. By clearing blockages in the liver and strengthening its energy, many of the vision problems correct.

Let's now look at kidney problems.

As you now know, kidney energy is the most important energy in the body. When people get sick, the first place that goes wrong is the kidney. When the kidney energy is not strong, the other parts of the body do not have enough energy to run. Part of the organs has to shut down, and the body will feel uncomfortable. When this situation goes on too long, physical sickness develops. That is why Chinese medicine pays great attention to kidney energy.

According to Chinese medicine, kidney system includes the two kidneys, which the Chinese call inner kidneys), the reproductive organs, which the Chinese call outer kidneys, the bladder, and the female breasts.

Follow this healing procedure for kidney healing:

1) Open #C7
2) Open the bottom of the feet. where the kidney energy channels begin.
3) Open the bottom of the torso, the point in between the two legs.
4) Open the tip of the tailbone. Open the lower back.
5) Open the point between the two kidneys.
6) After removing blockages out from these areas, you give energy back to the kidneys.

When you give energy to the kidneys, you can use your palms to give energy to the kidney. But quite often, I give energy back to the kidneys by using my sword fingers. Kidney energy belongs to Yin. Energy from sword fingers belongs to Yin, too. They match up very well.

There are other problems related to the kidneys.
In addition to what I just said, keep the following in mind:

- When your friend has breast problems, you must also open the areas under her arms and then move to her breasts.
- For Low sexual energy, focus more on the tailbone, the lower back, and the point between the two kidneys.
- For Sterility, focus more in the bottom of the feet, the tailbone, the bottom of the torso, the lower back.
- For reproductive organ problems the same as working on sterility
- For ringing in the ears, watering in the ears, weak hearing, work on the kidneys first before you come to the ears.
- For problems with Sterility or Fertility, work on the kidneys to strengthen the kidney energy.

After healing, you ask your friend to hit the tailbone with an empty fist several times a day for five to ten minutes each time.

Breast and Reproductive Organ Problems

For breast and reproductive organ problems, you may show your friend the breasts massage exercise. The breasts message exercise can help to open the channels in the breasts and reproductive organs, keep the channels open, and heal the body fast. It can also energize the body.

Now here is the technique to do the exercise:

1) Rub the hands until they are warm.
2) Hold the breasts by using the middle of the palms to touch the nipples.
3) Move your hands inward in a circular way 36 times.
4) Then move your hands outward 36 times.
5) While you are doing so, focus your mind in your heart.
6) Then hold your breasts and lift them up gently, and take a deep breath three times. While you are doing the exercise, you close your eyes. Wear a smile on your face.
7) Do the exercise in the morning or late afternoon. You can do it as many times as you like.

A lady was diagnosed with a pre-cancerous tumor in the ovary and her breasts were congested. She had an irregular menstrual cycle too. The tumor was five centimeters big. She was scheduled for surgery in one month.

She came to see me. After my healing I showed her the breast massage exercise. She did it two to three times a day. Plus I gave her a couple more healing sessions. She found the congestion in the breasts was gone. She went to the hospital to have a check up before surgery. The tumor was gone!

We know the breasts and the reproductive organs belong to the kidney energy system. When you massage the breasts it affects the reproductive organs too. That is why the congestion in the breasts went away and the reproductive organ was healed.

There are other organs and body parts that I did not mention. They do not require special instructions. Do the standard healing process on all areas of the body where you find blockages.

There may be time when your friend has diabetes, or high blood pressure, or constipation.

Let's now look at some of these conditions. There are things you can do to help your friend right away.

For diabetes and high and low blood sugar you will find blockages in these areas: kidneys, pancreas, liver and bladder. You need to clear blockages from all these areas. After that you comb the body down from the head to the feet by sending energy out through your fingers. With high blood sugar, the message you use is, *"ALL THE CHANNELS OPEN. BLOOD SUGAR DOWN TO NORMAL."* After that you give energy back to the MIDDLE Dantian.

Combing Energy

When your friend has low blood sugar, you comb the energy up from the feet to the head. The message is similar, *"ALL THE CHANNELS OPEN. BLOOD SUGAR UP TO NORMAL."*

Here is how you comb energy. Pay attention, because you will also use this process when your friend has high or low blood pressure or high cholesterol.

1) Stand in front or back of the person.
2) Raise your hands with fingers open from the sides of the person to the top of the head.
3) Comb the fingers down from the top to the feet. Remember to keep you hands about 20 inches from your friend's body.
4) Hold the energy blockages as extra energy in the body and return it back to the universe.
5) Repeat it as many times until you feel the blockage is gone. Repeat the message as you are doing the healing.
6) Give energy back to the Lower Dantian or Middle Dantian.

When your friend has high or low blood pressure you will find blockages in the liver and the heart, and the head. So you need to clear blockages out from all these areas. If you feel too hot in the areas, that mean this person has high blood pressure problem. If you feel too cold, that means low blood pressure problem.

Use the same combing techniques that we just talked about to deal with blood sugar.

The message you use in the healing is, *"ALL CHANNELS OPEN. BLOOD PRESSURE UP/DOWN TO NORMAL."*

I have a medical doctor friend who is a high blood pressure doctor. He heard about my class and he came to the class. He had high blood pressure. He practiced the exercise and later he came to me a few times for healing and the blood pressure was under control Now we became very good friends. With him we are helping to heal high blood pressure by using Qigong.

Heart Attacks

If you are with a friend when he has a heart attack, focus on the spine and the front channel. Open the small universe. Do not chase after the pain. As long as you can keep the back and front channels open, the pain will go away very soon.

Here I have a story to tell you. Once in my class, a licensed nurse was having a heart attack. The pain was radiating from the chest to the arms. She was crying. I asked one of my students who I had trained in my advanced class to come over to help her. First my student was very nervous. He chased after the pain, and more pain came. He was sweating. I saw that. I asked him not to focus on the pain, but the small universe. I told him that I was sending energy to him while he was working on her. So he did. He kept clearing blockages out from the spine and the front channels. Within a few minutes, the pain went away. His work helped stop a heart attack.

If you are helping a friend who had already had a heart attack, besides opening the back and front channel, focus on the top of the heart area. The rest of the healing technique is the same as you deal with general heart problems.

Does your friend have High Cholesterol?

Use sword fingers where you find blockages, and then use the same combing technique that we use for High Blood Pressure. The message is, *"ALL CHANNELS OPEN. CHOLESTEROL BACK TO NORMAL."*

How about Constipation?

First, make sure the bathroom is open. Then work on the lungs. Then come to the large intestines to clear the blockages. Ask your friend to drink Yin-Yang water.

Say the message to yourself, *"ALL CHANNELS OPEN. RECTUM COMPLETELY OPENS."*

And for Diarrhea?

Work on the liver, kidneys, and intestines.

Ask your friend to drink Yin-Yang water.

And use the Message, *"ALL CHANNELS OPEN. DIARRHEA COMPLETELY STOPS."*

If you are with a friend who has diarrhea, and you don't remember what to do, don't worry. Just do a full healing. Detect blockages, remove blockages, and put in fresh, healing energy. You will help stop the diarrhea right away. This is true for many other problems in the body.

Does your friend have a Cold, Flu, or Fever?

The first place for cold to start is in the bottom of the feet. So the first thing you need to do is to open the channels in the bottom of the feet--and tell him to keep his feet warm all of the time.

Then you come to open #C7, then the base of the head, the top of the head, the forehead, then the tips of the shoulders. Then go and open all of the other blockages you find.

If your friend has a fever, focus on the bottom of the feet and #C7 more.

If your friend is coughing, you can use sword fingers to briskly rub the inner parts of his arms for a couple of minutes – I demonstrate this on the video. Then remove blockages out from the arms.

If your friend has Arthritis:

Clear blockages from the pancreas first. When this part is congested, the energy might stick in the joints. Do you remember how problems with the shoulders and neck have their root in the pancreas? It is the same for other joints in the body, too.

Arthritis in the upper part of the torso, such as in the neck, shoulders, arms, etc., open #C7 before you come to the area where the arthritis is located.

Arthritis in the lower part of the torso, such as in the lower back, hips, legs, etc., open the lower back first before you clear blockages from the location of the arthritis.

Give energy back to the pancreas and Lower Dantian.

Say the Message, *"ALL CHANNELS OPEN. ARTHRITIS IS COMPLETELY HEALED!"*

What about Addictions (Smoking, Drinking, etc)?

If a person has an addiction, there must be some blockages in the liver. We know the internal energy starts at the Lower Dantian. When the energy (life force) in the Lower Dantian is getting stronger, it goes to the liver and changes into wisdom energy. When the energy in the liver is getting stronger, it travels up to the heart and changes into spiritual energy. When the spiritual energy in the heart gets strong, it travels up to the third eye and opens the third eye.

When the wisdom energy goes wrong, a person will make poor decisions in his or her life. Addictions are a part of it. Smoking, drinking, workaholic, etc. are symptoms of poor energy circulation in the liver.

So, when you help others with smoking, alcoholism, drug use, any addiction, you should clear energy blockages in the liver, then the Middle Dantian, and then the head.

With drug addictions you also need to clear blockages from the bone marrow and kidneys.

After you clear blockages in these energy centers, you show the Level One exercise "Moving of Yin and Yang" to your friend. Ask your friend to do this exercise once a day for half an hour. Also ask your friend to message his or her ears ten minutes a day, three times a day.

How do you handle missing or removed organs?

The same as if it is there. Even if an organ or limb is missing or has been removed, the energy channel is still present so send energy as if the organ were still there.

What about working on a pregnant friend?

Don't sweep energy down from the head to the legs. Move blockages out from the sides of the body. In this way you will not disturb the peace of the baby.

Addressing Specific Problems

Head

Always use Sword Fingers to open the following four areas for any problems in the head (such as headache, ear infection, eye problems, etc.). Do not put energy into the areas until all areas are opened.

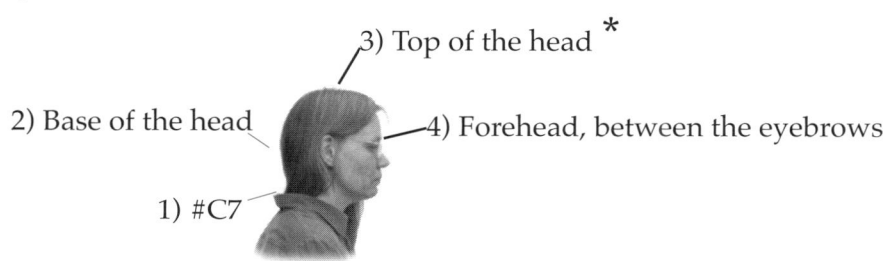

3) Top of the head *
2) Base of the head
4) Forehead, between the eyebrows
1) #C7

Then, follow the appropriate instructions below.
* Do not pull energy out directly from the top of the head. When you open the channel in the top of the head, energy comes out faster. Instead, remove the blocked energy out from the sides of the head.

Headache

- Use the Sword Fingers to open the whole neck spine. Clear blockages.
- Use Sword Fingers on the area where your friend feels pain or discomfort to open the blockage.
- Open your hands and visualize your fingers going into the area and take hold of the blockage as smoke, pull the smoke out, and throw it away.

Do not put energy into the head before you remove the blockages when a person has headache, because this does not help.

Eye Problems

When removing blockages from a friend with eye problems, say this to yourself, *"All of the blockages are gone. The function of the eye is completely back to normal."* Remember to give energy back to the areas with blockages.

- Open the points between each eye and the side of the bridge of the nose on both sides of the bridge of the nose.
- Remove blockages from the eye (or eyes) with the problem. (Remember to do the eye with the least blockage first.)
- Open the liver. Low liver energy affects vision.

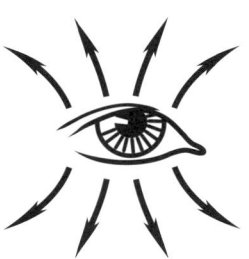

two points

Nearsightedness

- Remove the blockage by moving one hand up and the other hand down.

The pupil of a nearsighted eye is generally oval, so an alternative technique is to use Sword Fingers in a circular manner while visualizing the eye as round as the full moon.

Farsightedness

- Remove the blockage by pulling it directly from the front of the eye, because the focus of the eye goes deep into the eyes. When your friend has both nearsighted and farsighted problems, use the two techniques together.

Additional techniques for the eyes

- After all healing involving the eye, instruct your friend to do the three neck exercises from the Ending Exercise of the Level One Active Exercise. Two of these exercises use the chin to draw six or seven horizontal circles from left to right and then right to left. The third is to dolphin the neck six or seven times.
- Instruct your friend to massage the corners of her eyes.

- Instruct your friend to bend her neck forward and use the cupped-hand to pat the base of the head for two minutes.
- Instruct your friend to rub her hands until they are very warm. Cover the eyes for two minutes with the palms. Repeat three times. Ask her to repeat in her mind: *"My eyesight is back to normal. I am completely healed."*

These exercises can help keep the channels open so ask your friend to do them at least three times a day.

Weak Eyesight, Itching, Watering

Do the liver first, because weak eyesight, itching, and watering may be related to a blockage in the liver.

Cross-eye Problems, Cataracts

Work on the same areas as other eye problems, but pay more attention to the neck, the base of the head, and the two points on the two sides of the bridge of the nose.

Ear Problems

Remember to open the four points in the head before working on any blockages in the head. When working on the ears, always do the ear with the least blockage first and always put energy back in the body.

Ear Infection

- Open the areas in front of the ears.

Hearing Loss, Ringing in the Ear, Water in the Ear

- Open the kidneys following the instructions found later, because hearing problems are often associated with weak kidney energy.
- Open the four points in the head.
- Open the areas in front of the ears.
- Ask your friend to strengthen the kidney energy through the Active Exercise from Level One.
- Ask your friend to get plenty of sleep.

Ringing in the ears when caused by loud noise does not originate with the kidneys.

Deafness caused from Aging
- Open the kidneys.
- Go back and open the base of the head again.
- Open the areas in front of the ears.
- Use your middle fingers to press in the front part of the ears so that air cannot flow into the ears. Hold in this position for about five minutes. Repeat in your mind, "The hearing ability comes back, completely." Move your fingers away quickly. If at the moment your friend hears the sound "Pong," the channels will be 80% open, and hearing improves.

Deafness caused by Medication or Fever

Follow the instructions for deafness caused from aging. Deafness caused from nerve damage, however, is very difficult to help.

Nose problems

Nose problems including stuffy nose, sinus problems, bloody nose, soar throat, and dry throat are associated with lung energy. Always give energy back to the body after you clear the blockages.
- Open the lungs first, because all nose and throat problems relate to blockages in the lungs.
- For a bloody nose, open the gallbladder and pancreas.
- Open the four points in the head. For sinus problems and stuffy nose, focus more on the base of the head and the forehead.
- Open any other blockages in the head.

When your friend has sinus problems have him stand, sit, or lie down with his arms above his head for two or three minutes.

Teeth Problems
- After opening the four points in the head, use Sword Fingers in circular motions around the closed mouth to open all of the teeth channels.

After you clear blockages in the teeth for a toothache, do not put energy in. The palm's energy is Yang, and the teeth's energy is Yin. I always put energy back into the area where I removed a blockage except for a toothache.

TMJ (Temporomandibular Joint Problem)
- After opening the four points of the head, focus on the neck and the base of the head, which has the main blockage for TMJ.
- Open the areas in front of the ears where the joints of the jaw meet. Say to yourself, "All of the joints are open. Completely healed!"

Facial Pain
- After opening the four points of the head, clear blockages from the neck spine.
- Use Sword Fingers to break the energy magnetic field of the pain area. Say in your mind: "Pain is gone. Completely healed!"

Shoulders and Neck
- Open the C7 vertebra.
- Open the pancreas. Remember to open the relative part of the spine first and to give energy back to the body.

Most of the tightness and pain in the shoulders and neck is from the energy imbalance in the pancreas. When the pancreas is congested, energy blocks in the shoulder and does not flow freely, which results in tightness and pain.

(Injuries, however, are not related to the pancreas.)

- Open the blockages in the shoulder or neck. When doing the shoulders, remember to do the shoulder with the least blockage first.

Lungs

These instructions refer to all aspects of the breathing system including coughing, congestion in the lungs, skin, and large intestines.

- Open the C7 vertebra.
- Open the relative area on the spine.
- Open the areas under the collar bones, which are called the "windows to the lungs."
- Do Sword Fingers on both lungs, starting with the lung with the least blockage.
- Remove blockages using this special technique: stand in front or behind your friend; open your two hands; move the hands down from the shoulders to the bottom of the lungs; and at the same time clear the blockages from the outer layers to the inner layers. Repeat this as many times until you feel the blockages are clear.
- After the healing ask your friend to hold his arms above the head with fingers open for ten minutes or more, three or more times a day.
- Ask your friend to cup the "windows to the lungs" for several minutes.
- Show your friend how to do the Active Exercise from Level One, especially "Breathing of the Universe." These exercises will help keep the channels open and help the lungs heal faster.
- Ask your friend to massage his thumbs for two to three minutes several times each day.

Heart

- Open the C7 vertebra.
- Open the relative area on the spine.
- Smile from your heart. It is especially important that you smile when working on your friend's heart.
- Use your palm to pump energy into the heart.
- Use Sword Fingers on the heart from the back or from the sides. Do not use Sword Fingers directly from the front to the heart, because the Sword Finger energy is more Yin (negative) and the heart's energy is more Yang (positive). The heart rejects Sword Finger energy coming from the front.
- Remove blockages from either the front or the back. Move both hands in the shape of a heart. Repeat, moving from the outside of the heart in. When removing energy from the heart, palm energy into the heart frequently.
- Do a healing on the small intestines, which are related to the heart. Open the relative area on the spine first and remember to give it energy.
- After your healing, ask your friend to massage her middle and little fingers for ten minutes three times a day. Noon is the best time, because the heart channels automatically open each day at noon; noon is also a good time to do a heart healing. Active Exercise from Level One, such as "Moving of Yin and Yang" and "Joining of Yin and Yang" are good for heart problems.
- You may also ask your friends to tap her fingers on the table for several minutes a day as if playing the piano. This can also help people with Alzheimer's.

(Pacemakers do not affect the healing.)

Liver
- Open the C7 vertebra.
- Open the relative area on the spine.
- Open the liver, and give energy to the liver.
- Open the gallbladder. When the liver has extra energy, the energy goes to the gallbladder and changes into bile, which is used to help digest the food.
- Open the pancreas, which works closely with the liver.

Blocked liver energy travels to the heart and could cause a heart attack, and it could travel to the brain and cause a stroke.

Kidneys

Kidney energy is the most important energy in the body. Strong kidney energy gives a person strong arms, a strong voice, strong sexual energy, and wisdom. Weak kidney energy affects the entire body and can lead to long, physical illness.

According to Chinese medicine, the kidney system includes the two kidneys (Chinese call them inner kidneys), the reproductive organs (Chinese call them outer kidneys), the bladder, and the breasts.

The healing procedure for kidney healing:
- Open the C7 vertebra.
- Open the bottom of the feet. Chinese call these two points "Bubbling Spring," where the kidney energy channels begin.
- Open the bottom of the torso, which is the point in between the two legs.
- Open the tip of the tailbone.
- Open the lower back.
- Open the point between the two kidneys.
- Give energy to the kidneys by using your palm or by using Sword Fingers.

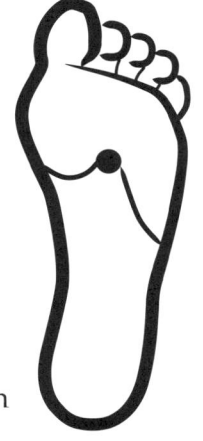

I often use Sword Fingers to give energy to the kidneys, because kidney energy is Yin and so is Sword Fingers energy.

Female Breasts

Follow the above steps for healing the kidneys, then:

- Open the areas under your friend's arms.
- Open the area of the spine relative to the breasts.
- Open each breast, beginning with the breast with the least blockage.
- After healing ask your friend to hit the tailbone with an empty fist in the morning for one to two minutes.
- Ask your friend to stand for twenty minutes a day holding her arms around an invisible beach ball or laundry basket with knees bent.
- Ask your friend to massage the "lung point," which is located a palm's width below the underarm area, especially if the area is sore.

I strongly recommend that your friend do the following breast massage daily. The best times are in the early morning or late afternoon. In the morning the lung energy channels are open. In late afternoon the kidney channels are open. When you massage the breasts at these times, it not only helps the breasts, but also helps the lungs and kidneys.

- Hold the breasts by using the middle of the palms to touch the nipples.
- Close your eyes, smile, and focus your mind in your heart.
- Move your hands inward in a circular way 36 times. Be gentle, but quick.
- Move your hands outward in a circular way 36 times.
- Hold your breasts and lift them up gently, taking three deep breaths.

Areas related to the Kidneys

The following problems are associated with weak kidney energy. Do a complete kidney healing in addition to the following:

Low sexual energy
Focus more on the tailbone, the lower back, and the point between the two kidneys.

Sterility
Focus more on the bottom of the feet, the tailbone, the bottom of the torso, and the lower back.

Reproductive organ problems
Focus more on the bottom of the feet, the tailbone, the bottom of the torso, and the lower back. Women should do the breast massage, especially when their menstrual period is irregular or too long. Men should massage the tailbone and the bottom of the torso with their middle finger.

Fertility, Immune System, Bladder
Strengthen the kidney energy.

Diabetes (High and Low Blood Sugar)

- If your friend has high blood sugar have her sit with her palms facing down. If your friend has low blood sugar, have her sit with her palms facing up.
- Open the C7 vertebra.
- Clear the kidneys, pancreas, liver, and bladder. Remember to open the relative area on the spine and to give energy back to the body.
- Stand in front or back of your friend. Raise your hands with your fingers open to the top of your friend's head if she has high blood sugar.
- Comb the fingers down to the feet.
- Say to yourself, *"All the channels open. Blood sugar down to normal. Diabetes completely healed."*

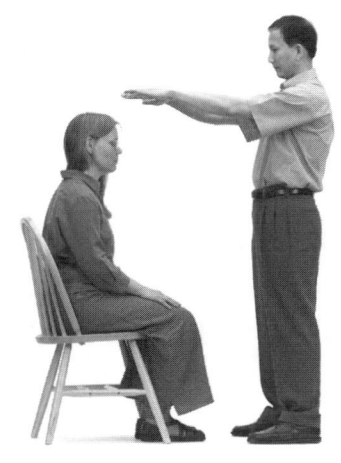 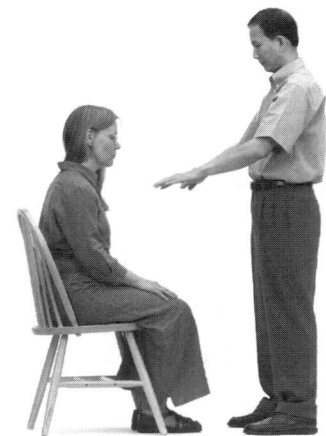

• Hold the energy blockages as extra energy in the body and return it back to the universe.
• Repeat it as many times as you feel until the blockage is removed.
• Give energy back to the lower Dantian.

For low blood sugar, comb from the bottom up and say to yourself, *"All the channels open. Blood sugar up to normal."*

• After the healing, ask your friend to massage the sides of the index and ring fingers several times a day for three to five minutes each. Massage from top down to lower blood sugar and from bottom up to raise blood sugar.

High and Low Blood Pressure

• If your friend has high blood pressure have him sit with his palms facing down. If your friend has low blood pressure, have him sit with his palms facing up.
• Open the liver, heart, and the head. When your friend has high blood pressure, you will feel warmth in these areas. When your friend has low blood pressure, you will feel coolness.
• Use the same combing technique used for people with high or low blood sugar. Say to yourself, *"All channels open. Blood pressure up/down to normal."*

• After the healing, ask your friend to massage the sides of the middle and little fingers for ten minutes several times a day. Massage from top down to lower blood pressure and from bottom up to raise blood pressure.

High Cholesterol

• Open the liver, heart, and the head. Say to yourself, *"All channels open. Cholesterol back to normal."*
• Use the same technique as high blood pressure. Have your friend sit with her palms down.

Heart Attack

• Open the spine and the front energy channel when someone is having a heart attack. Do not chase after the pain. As long as you can keep the back and front channels open, you can help the pain subside.
• Use your thumbnail to press in on the tip of your friend's index fingers for one minute.
• After you have completed your healing, after the heart attack has passed and your friend is recovering have your friend massage her/his middle and little fingers for five to ten minutes.

Constipation

• Work on the lungs, kidneys, bottom of feet, and heels.
• Open the large intestines. Say to yourself, *"All channels open. Rectum completely open."*
• Visualize the intestines opening. Use an outward sweeping motion to move away excess energy.
• Ask your friend to drink Yin-Yang water as described in Level One. Yin-Yang water is half boiled water, half spring water, mixed together. Let it cool, and drink while still warm.

Diarrhea

• Work on the liver, kidneys, and intestines. Say to yourself, *"All channels open. Diarrhea completely stops."*

- Visualize the intestines closing. Use an inward sweeping motion to move away excess energy.
- Ask your friend to drink Yin-Yang water.

Weak liver energy diminishes the body's ability to digest food. Asking your friend to focus in the lower Dantian can help calm the digesting system and reduce nausea.

Digestion
- Open the liver, gallbladder, and intestines.
- Ask your friend to drink Yin-Yang water.

When the liver has extra energy, the energy goes to the gallbladder and changes into bile, which is used to help digest the food. When a person's liver is good, his digesting is also good.

Cold, Flu, Fever, Sinus Problems, Asthma, and Emphysema
- Open the channels in the bottom of the feet.
- Open the C7 vertebra, base of the head, top of the head, forehead, and the tips of the shoulders.
- If your friend has a fever, focus on the bottom of the feet and the area around the C7 vertebra.
- For coughing, use Sword Fingers to briskly and firmly rub the inner parts of her arms until a blue color shows. And then remove blockages out from the arms.

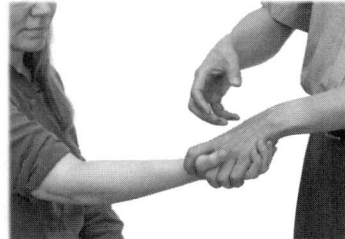

Cold, Flu, Fever, Sinus Problems, Asthma, and Emphysema (continued)

- Ask your friend to keep her feet warm and massage her feet and the top of her head for twenty minutes each day. She should also pat the torso like the Ending Exercise of Level One and massage the tips of the shoulder if they are sore.
Review the Lungs section for additional insight.

Pregnancy and Menstrual Period

When you are working with a pregnant friend or a woman having her period, keep these guidelines in mind.
- Never pull energy down the body. Instead, go to the sides.
- Instead of giving energy to the lower Dantian, give energy to the middle Dantian, which is the heart center.
- Have your friend focus in her heart during the healing session, if possible

Warts
- Open the C7 vertebra.
- Open the heart channels.
- Use Sword Fingers on the wart.

Arthritis

- Clear blockages from the pancreas, because energy often "sticks" in the joints when the pancreas becomes congested.
- For arthritis in the upper part of the torso, such as in the neck, shoulders, arms, etc., open the C7 vertebra before you clear the blockages in the area of the arthritis. When clearing blockages in the arms, conduct the energy down from the shoulders to the elbows and out through the hands.
- Say to yourself, "All channels open. Arthritis is completely healed."
- For arthritis in the lower part of the torso, such as in the lower back, hips, legs, etc., open the lower back before you clear the blockages in the area of the arthritis.
- Give energy to the pancreas and lower Dantian.

Addictions (Smoking, Drinking, Drug Use, etc)

- Clear blockages in the liver, then the Middle Dantian, and then the head.
- For drug use clear the blockages in the bone marrow and kidneys as well.
- After clearing blockages in these energy centers, you show the Level One exercise "Moving of Yin and Yang" to your friend.
- Ask your friend to do this exercise once a day for half an hour.
- Also ask your friend to message his or her ears ten minutes a day, three times a day

If a person has an addiction, there must be some blockages in the liver. We know the internal energy starts at the Lower Dantian. When the energy (life force) in the Lower Dantian is getting stronger, it goes to the liver and changes into wisdom energy. When the energy in the liver is getting stronger, it travels up to the heart and changes into spiritual energy. When the spiritual energy in the heart gets strong, it travels up to the third eye and opens the third eye.

When the wisdom energy goes wrong, a person will make poor decisions in his or her life. Addictions are a part of it. Smoking, drinking, workaholic, etc. are symptoms of poor energy circulation in the liver.

The Active Exercises

Level One Active Exercises strengthen your physical energy, open your energy channels, and balance your body's energy.

Level Two Active Exercises help increase your healing energy and develop your visualization.

You can practice either set of exercises. When you have noticed improvements in your physical condition, you can replace Level One exercises with Level Two exercises. You may want to revisit Level One exercises when you become ill or involved in an accident.

Continue with the Small Universe Sitting Meditation, because it is valuable for increasing healing energy. For maximum benefit I recommend that you practice Spring Forest Qigong one to two hours every day.

Now we are going to discuss the four simple exercises or movements of Level Two.

All the active exercises of Level Two are designed to help you increase your healing power and develop your spirituality. These exercises will also help you with your own health just as the movements in Level One do. You can do either the exercises in Level One or Level Two for your own health purposes; or you can choose to do all of them if you have time; or you can combine them together. There is no one way. They are all beneficial.

Practicing the Exercises of Level Two

The four active exercises are

- *Sword fingers*
- *Thunder palms*
- *10,000 hands*
- *Cloud hands*

You can practice these movements for any period of time. Two minutes or ten minutes or 90 minutes. You can practice them together or separately. Of course, the more you practice all four movements, the stronger your energy and the stronger your ability to heal.

As I mentioned earlier, there is also a 30 minute audio session available on which we practice all four movements and I also demonstrate the movements on the video tapes.

Before a practice session, stand in the open Qigong pose and bounce on the balls of your feet for two minutes. This will help loosen the energy in your body and will make your practice more effective.

Always say the password: *"I am in the universe. The universe in my body. The universe and I combine together."* This will help you connect to the pure universal energy, which as you remember from Level One is key to the success of Spring Forest Qigong.

When you go into the emptiness, you forget about your worries, your cares, your blockages and you experience love, euphoria, peace, and balance. It is wonderful.

1 - Sword Fingers Practice

To help increase your healing energy and develop your visualization. To help heal blockages in the lungs and digesting system and strengthen the kidney energy.

The quality of the energy sent out from the Sword Fingers is Yin. We use this type of energy to break out the energy blockages, the blocked magnetic field.

To increase your healing power, visualize the energy coming out the Sword Fingers like a laser beam. It penetrates everything in its way including walls, trees, and hills. When the energy meets a stone visualize the stone exploding.

---

1) Stand in regular Qigong exercise pose. Bend your knees a little. If you want to lose weight, bend your knees more. In this way you can help open the belt channel around the waist and the kidney channel faster.

2) Raise your arms out in front of you horizontally at about shoulder height, keeping them shoulder width apart. Let your elbows drop a little. The palms should face each other.

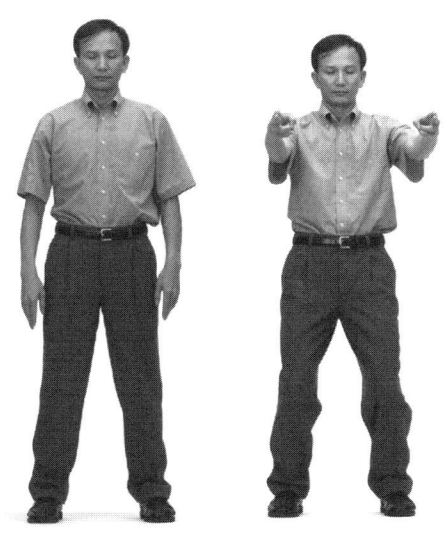

Sword Fingers continued

3) Hold your fingers in the Sword Fingers position from Level 1. That is, put the index and middle fingers together and point forward. The ring and little fingers are curled in towards the palm with the pad of the thumb placed over them —this forms a circle on each hand with the two fingers and thumb.

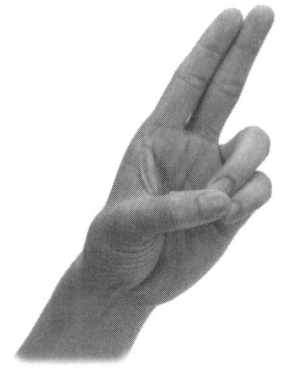

4) Inhale, pulling energy from the universe through every cell in the body. The energy collects in the middle Dantian, which is under the bottom of the heart, or it collects in the lower Dantian, which is deep in behind the navel. Collecting the energy in the middle Dantian can be more powerful.

5) Exhale, saying "ohmmmm…" in a low tone, as you imagine the sound coming from the heart. Energy flows out the tips of your sword fingers to the end of the universe.

6) Repeat the inhale/exhale cycle.

As a beginner you can say the "ohmmm…" sound in a very low tone. But when you practice more and deeper, you do not need to say it aloud. You can chant the sound in your heart and visualize saying the tone aloud. If you feel strain in your back, arms, or shoulders, rest your arms for a few seconds.

2 - Thunder Palms Practice

To help increase your healing energy and develop your visualization. To help heal blockages in the heart

This exercise trains you to send out energy from the palms. The quality of this energy is Yang. We use this technique to pass healing energy to the body after we remove the blockages. (The Thunder Palm posture is used only when you practice this exercise. When you pass energy into a friend's body, you do not need to hold the Thunder Palm posture. Instead, open your hands with your fingers slightly apart and send energy to the body.)

---

1) Stand in the pose as you do for Sword Fingers practice.

2) After you finish the exercise Sword Fingers, gently lower your arms and open your fingers. Then raise your arms out in front of you to shoulder height, elbows bent a little. Bend your wrists up so that your palms are facing forward. Thumb and index fingers point up, middle, ring and little fingers curl in towards but not touching the palm.

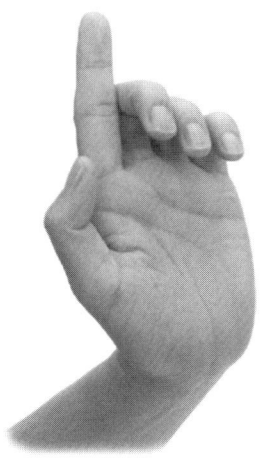

Thunder Palms continued

3) Inhale, pulling energy from the universe through every cell in the body and collecting energy in the middle Dantian, which is your heart center.

4) Exhale, saying "ohmmmmm…" in a low tone while visualizing bright and colorful energy flowing out from the middle of the palms of your hands to the end of the universe.

5) Repeat the inhale/exhale cycle.

When you hold your hands in this posture, drop your elbows. Stand still; do not move your body so that energy flows uninterrupted.

As a beginner you can say the "ohmmm-mmmm…" sound in a very low tone. When you practice more and deeper, you do not need to say it aloud. You can chant the sound in your heart and imagine saying the tone aloud. If you feel strain in your back, arms, or shoulders, rest your arms for a few seconds.

3 - 10,000 Hands Practice

To help develop your spiritual energy and purify your soul energy. To help heal blockages in the lungs, digesting system, liver, and intestines.

As you do this movement, visualize 10,000 hands coming out of your body and moving together in the same direction as your hands. Imagine each of these 10,000 hands gathering spiritual energy and increasing your own spiritual energy.

While you are doing this movement you might smell the fragrance of beautiful flowers.

Chant "Ohmmmmm..." to yourself as you exhale, visualizing the sound coming directly from your heart.

On each inhale, imagine universal energy coming into every cell of your body, collecting in the lower Dantian. With each exhale, imagine the energy shooting out from every part of the body to the end of the universe.

Do not move your spine from side to side, even when you feel tired, because that movement stops your energy from going to the emptiness level.

---

1) Stand in the same pose as you do in Sword Fingers.

10,000 Hands continued

2) Inhale as your arms sweep out from your sides and up in an arc.

3) Hands (palms) come together over your head, fingers pointing up.

4) Lower joined hands to touch the top of your head, fingers still pointing up. Pause for three seconds.

5) Exhale as you lower your joined hands down past your forehead. Fingers turn to face down as you pass your heart.

6) Stretch your joined hands down to the bottom of your torso while you are still exhaling.

7) Repeat

4 - Cloud Hands Practice

To help increase your visualization and healing power. To help increase your spiritual energy. While doing this exercise you may also notice you smell the fragrance of beautiful flowers. (Cloud Hands also helps develop the ability to help heal others long distance, a technique discussed in Level Three.)

By moving your hands out and in in the Cloud Hands movement and combining the breathing technique, you open blockages in the whole body, especially the lungs.

---

1) Stand in regular Qigong exercise pose.

2) Extend one arm with your hand open at shoulder level. Visualize reaching out your hand to the end of the universe and grasping a piece of beautiful, colorful cloud. Pull it toward you, and put it around you. Make sure your fingers are always open because when you open your fingers, you open energy channels; when you close your fingers, you close channels.

3) Repeat with other hand, and continue, alternating arms in a fluid motion.

Chant the sound "Ohmmmmm…" as you do in 10,000 Hands. Take deep and soft breaths by using the lower abdomen breathing technique. You can match your breathing with the movements, but it is not necessary.

5 - Ending: Harvesting of Qi

To adjust energy in the body and to help the body heal and gain back its energy balance faster.

All of the movements of the Active Exercises can be practiced separately. You might choose one or two movements each day, or you can do them all. Always finish with the Ending exercise. this will bring you out of your meditation and help put the Qi into the right places of your body. When you choose to follow your Active Exercise practice with a Sitting Meditation, do the Ending exercise after the Sitting Meditation.

1) Rub your hands together palm to palm.

2) Massage your face: with your palms toward your face use your middle fingers to push up along the bridge of the nose until your fingers reach the forehead; cover the face with your hands; and part your hands as they draw down the face to the chin.

3) Comb your head with your fingers from front to the back of the head. The tips of your fingers must touch your scalp.

4) Massage your ears from top to bottom. Every part of the ear must be massaged.

Virtual Compass

Our body is a virtual compass; we can make our meditations more effective by aligning ourselves with the universe before we begin.

1) Stand with your feet less than shoulder-width apart, arms relaxed at your side, hands relaxed, and fingers open. Move your elbows out a little.

2) Relax your body, pull your chin back to straighten your spine, place your tongue on the roof of your mouth, and close your eyes.

3) Connect with universal energy by saying in your mind the password: "I am in the universe. The universe is in my body. The universe and I combine together."

4) Call upon your master's energy. Ask the universe for the best direction to face while you meditate at this time. You may say, "Master, please send me energy to help me find the best direction to practice Qigong today." Then you just stand still waiting patiently with a smile on your face.

5) When you feel a force coming to move you, let it happen. You may be directed to step forward, backwards, sideways, and/or turn left or right. Keep moving until your body feels centered and your energy balanced. Your body will stop by itself.

Do this each time you meditate, because the best direction to face will likely vary each time.

You can also use this technique to find your way or to find people and things—it connects you with universal energy and universal knowledge.

Other forms of Qigong want people to face different directions at different times of the day. For instance, some masters ask their students to face east in the morning and north in the evening; some masters say we should face west in the morning and south in the afternoon; and some say you can face any direction. This can be confusing. Many people do not know which direction is right. Masters emphasize the importance of direction because our body is affected by the energy from the earth, sun, moon, planets, and objects around us. We want to create a harmonious environment to do meditation so that it is easy for us to go into the emptiness and open our energy channels.

Every body is a "small universe" with its own system. For one person, it may be good to face south when doing meditation, but for another person, it may be good only to face north.

To find the best direction for your meditation or exercise, use your body as a virtual compass. As a result, you will spend less time and get more benefit.

Sitting Postures

Different sitting postures help to conduct the flow of energy in the body

Specific sitting postures are not required when practicing the Sitting Meditations in Levels 1 and 2. Those who want to go up to an increasingly higher level of practice should train to do meditation in the full Lotus position.

At any level and with any posture, you need to keep the spine straight during meditation. This opens the governing channel–the back channel–along the spine and helps the kidney (life force) energy flow. Additionally, sitting with your legs crossed shuts off energy to the legs causing the energy to move up the torso and building wisdom energy.

Let's review the traditional Eastern styles of sitting:

1) Sitting/kneeling on your feet.

This position starts as kneeling, but you sit back so that your thighs are resting on your lower legs, top of your foot on floor, soles of your feet facing upward (typical Japanese sitting style). This position keeps your back straight and so helps open channels in the feet, especially the kidney channels. It is good for kidney stones and poor circulation in the lower abdomen.

2) Freestyle Lotus.

Sitting with legs crossed. Westerners may know this as sitting "Indian style."

3) Semi-Lotus.

Sitting with legs crossed, one foot placed on top of other leg (sole up).

4) Full Lotus.

Sitting with legs crossed, both feet on top of other leg, both soles facing up. This is the most desirable position; it opens the most channels and is the most stable. The closer you get to this position, the more your lower spine opens up, making your entire body more flexible. The lower spine is the location of your sacrum, which controls the flexibility of the body.

Full lotus sitting is preferred because it allows the body to stay in the emptiness the longest. Beginner's legs might go to sleep or feel painful. To reduce pain and to go into the emptiness, keep your body as still as you can without rocking. As you open your channels, your flexibility returns.

You might practice full lotus sitting while watching TV to divert your attention from pain or numbness.

Flexibility Exercises for Sitting Postures

The following exercises can help build flexibility to make it easier to sit in the Lotus position. I demonstrate them on the video.

1) Swing the torso similar to the neck exercise in the Ending Exercises of Level One. Do it nine times in each direction with your legs shoulder width apart. Then do it nine times in each direction with your legs together.

2) Put your hands on your knees. Swing your knees inwardly in a circle nine times.

3) Then swing your knees nine times outwardly.

4) Swing each ankle in a circular motion nine times in each direction.

Be patient. Allow your body the time to work up to sitting in the Full Lotus. Please remember that while wonderful benefits come from using the Full Lotus sitting position for your meditations, you do not need to be able to sit in a Full Lotus to be a powerful healer.

Hand Postures

The following hand postures control the flow of energy.

Open Hands

Keeping your hands open with your fingers spread, but not stretched, allows energy to flow in and out. Use this posture at the beginning of your meditation and healing session.

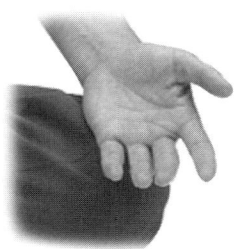

When the hands open, the energy channels in the hands open. The energy flows in and out of the body easily making it easier to get the blockages out of the body.

When you breathe, focus your attention on the skin and not on your nose or lungs. You will find that energy flows so easily in and out of the body.

Thumb and forefingers joined in circle

Holding your thumbs against your forefingers (ie, index fingers) is the "protection posture." It keeps your energy in and other's energy out.

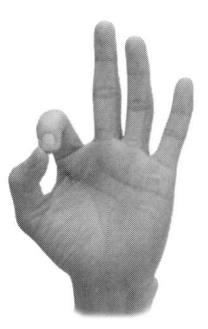

When you feel your energy is running out of your body, or when you feel someone is taking your energy away from your body, you can hold this posture. When you hold this posture, all of the energy channels in the body close. Energy can come in, but no energy escapes.

- You may use this posture when you are chilled to retain heat as long as possible.
- You may also use this posture when you experience fear, because it keeps your energy from draining.

As you hold this posture and call upon your master's energy, your aura changes when the spiritual energy comes to help you.

Black Sesame Seeds

Black sesame seeds help rebuild kidney energy, which aids in weight loss and improves the body's overall beauty and hair condition. Black sesame seeds also help heal cancer and kidney diseases.

- Soak two to three tablespoons of black sesame seeds in water for five minutes
- Discard floating seeds and hulls.
- Cook the remaining seeds for five minutes in one glass of water
- Let stand for 10 minutes
- Drink the broth and eat the seeds.
- You can make a large batch and keep in the refrigerator for up to a week.
- You can drink the broth daily. Morning is best.

Closing Thoughts

I would like to emphasize again that techniques are important in healing, but the source of healing power is not techniques. The healing power is from love, forgiveness, and kindness. If you have no love from the bottom of your soul, you cannot become a good healer, even when you know all these techniques, because you have no power to use them.

Never argue when you do healing with a friend. Maintain a pure heart. Do not consider yourself as a savior; consider yourself a friend helping a friend. Use each healing as an opportunity for you to grow. Always thank your friend for giving you the opportunity to practice what you have learned. Be grateful to your friend.

When you do healing, do not worry about your success or failure. Go do your work. Do your best.

Do not expect anything from your friend in return. The universe will know who you are. It will reward you in its own way.

When you use your Qigong skills to help someone heal, consider it an opportunity for sharing your universal love, forgiveness, and kindness with your friend. Consider it as a chance to pass this beautiful healing message to the world.

Qigong is a way to help awaken the natural healing ability that everyone has within themselves. Practicing Qigong can help bring about a complete healing of mind, body and spirit. As a Spring Forest Qigong practitioner you can help others to heal; but please remember, do not promise that you can heal anyone. Let yourself become an empty vessel, and let the universal energy flow through you to perform the complete healing. You just do your best and let the universe do the rest.

For some people, many people, Qigong works well. For some people with critical problems, it might take a longer time to help them. If your friend is in a very late stage, it might just help to reduce the pain, because the life force is leaving the body as will ultimately happen to us all.

Many people use what I teach in Level Two to help heal themselves. You might do Sword Fingers on any blockages you have after doing a Small Universe Sitting Meditation. Pull out the excess energy just as you would when you do a healing on someone else. You can then either use your palm to put energy into the area or bring in energy through your breathing.

My friend, thank you so much for walking with me on the path of sending universal love to our families, our friends, and all the people around us. And I am so happy that you and I can work together to make the world a better, healing, loving place to live. Thank you.

> *A healer in every family.*
> *A world without pain.*

Important Legal Warnings

State and Federal laws in the United States are very strict. Practicing Qigong healing might be considered practicing medicine without a license. We strongly suggest adhering to these guidelines:

• Do not use the word "diagnose." Only licensed medical professionals (physicians, acupuncturists, chiropractors, etc.) are legally entitled to diagnose illness. You "detect energy blockages."

• Refer to "blockages," not diseases, such as cancer, leukemia, fibermyalgia, etc. These are diagnostic words and Qigong practitioners do not diagnose.

• Do not refer to "cures." You cannot claim to cure someone. You can only help a person to heal himself or herself.

• Do not make "referrals" to medical practitioners. This implies that you have done a diagnosis. Instead suggest that the person may find another modality helpful.

• Never tell someone that a Qigong healing or Qigong practice is a replacement for any medical treatment they may be receiving. Qigong can be used as a complementary practice for medical care—not as a replacement

• Never tell someone to change or discontinue current medical treatment. Encourage them to seek advice from their physician or licensed health care practitioner.

On Discontinuing Medications

When the body no longer needs medication, such as insulin or allergies medicine, the body will start to reject them. You may notice they begin to taste terrible. When this happens, consult with the doctor who wrote the prescription to be retested. It is important to not stop medications prematurely or without your doctor's knowledge. Some medications require a supervised weaning process. Discuss all medication concerns with your doctor.

Acknowledgments

I would like to express my deep thanks:

To my Masters and spiritual guides
for all they have imparted to me.

To my wife, Fang, and son, Ming,
for all their love and support.

To Darcie Barrett for her joyful assistance
in preparing the information for this manual.

To Gary Rebstock for helping to create this manual
and for his invaluable assistance in producing and directing
the videotapes.

To all of my students for all the joy they have given me and
for giving me the opportunity to share the healing energy of
Qigong with them.

To all of the many others who helped make this manual
possible.

Additional Spring Forest Qigong Learning Materials

To learn more about Spring Forest Qigong please visit our websites at:

www.springforestqigong.com or www.bornahealer.com

Level 1 for Health

Video – In this 60-minute videotape, Master Lin guides you through all of the Active Exercises for Level 1 and shows you how to use the simple, yet powerful, "Sword Fingers" technique for helping others. Also on the tape, several of Master Lin's students tell of the remarkable healing experiences they have had with Spring Forest Qigong.

Manual – Includes detailed descriptions and illustrations of each of the Active Exercise movements for this level. It also explains the two Sitting Meditations for Level 1, "Small Universe" and Self-Concentration and how to use the "Sword Fingers" technique for helping others. In the manual you will also learn: How Energy Blockages Are Formed, How to Awaken Your Natural Healing Abilities, and the Keys to Your Success.

Exercise & Meditation Audio Cassettes – This is a set of two cassette tapes. One is an audio guide to the Level 1 Active Exercises. On the other cassette, Master Lin guides you through the "Small Universe" and "Self-Concentration" meditations with beautiful and soothing background music.

Lecture Audio Cassettes – This is a set of four cassette tapes. Master Lin discusses how to bring the power of Spring Forest Qigong into your life. Topics include: The Miracle of Qi Energy, The Secrets of Qigong, Exploring the Active Exercises, Understanding Sitting Meditations, and Helping Others to Heal.

Inner Beauty Meditation CD – This original meditative music, designed by Master Lin, is a unique blending of traditional Chinese and contemporary music. It is designed to enhance your meditation experience.

Level II for Healing

Videos – This is a set of two, hour-long videotapes. Master Lin shows you step-by-step how to use more advanced Spring Forest Qigong techniques to help others to heal. You will learn how to Detect Energy Blockages, how to Open the Small Universe for Others, how to Increase Your Own Healing Energy and much more.

Manual – Includes all of the information presented in the videotapes in a step-by-step, easy to follow format. It is an invaluable reference guide for anyone wanting to use Spring Forest Qigong techniques to help others.

Lecture Audio Cassettes – This is a set of three cassettes. The subjects Master Lin discusses include: Becoming a Successful Healer, Three Secrets to Qigong Healing, Special Qigong Healing Techniques and more.

Back Into the Universe Meditation CD – Master Lin designed this music to focus on helping you go even deeper into the meditative experience, to help you connect more deeply than ever before with the Emptiness and enhance your feelings of relaxation and peacefulness.

Small Universe CD – The Small Universe meditation helps to powerfully open and connect the front energy channel (Yin Mai) and the back channel (Du Mai or Governing channel). According to Chinese medicine, if a person can keep these two channels open all of the time, she/he will have no energy blockage in the body. This hour-long meditation will help you open these two channels and stay longer in the meditation. This can help you cultivate more internal Qi, strengthen your energy and develop your energy centers.

Level III

Sun Meditation CD – This CD is designed for use by Level III students. Master Lin guides you through this meditation which helps the student open the "third eye." Sun and Moon meditations are designed to compliment each other. Sun Meditation helps us open the energy centers and cultivates the physical energy in the energy centers.

Moon Meditation CD – This CD is designed for use by Level III students. Master Lin guides you through this meditation which helps the student open the "third eye." Moon and Sun meditations are designed to compliment each other. Moon Meditation helps soothe the energy and helps develop spiritual energy.

Level IV

Rainbow Meditation CD – This CD is designed for use by Level IV students. It helps you open all the channels in the body, bring energy to every cell, develop the third eye and your spiritual energy, and helps heal bone marrow problems.

All Spring Forest Qigong Learning Materials are available through our websites:

www.springforestqigong.com

or

www.bornahealer.com

Notes

Notes